A PHILOSOPHER'S COMPASS

A PHILOSOPHER'S COMPASS

Jonathan Jacobs
Colgate University

Australia • Canada • Mexico • Singapore • Spain
United Kingdom • United States

Publisher: Earl McPeek
Executive Editor: David Tatom
Market Strategist: Adrienne Krysiuk
Project Editor: Katherine Dennis
Art Director: Vicki Whistler
Production Manager: Linda McMillan

Cover image: Courtesy of Photodisk

ISBN: 0-15-507543-8

Library of Congress Catalog Card Number: 00-101983

Wadsworth/Thomson Learning
10 Davis Drive
Belmont CA 94002-3098
USA

For information about our products, contact us:
Thomson Learning Academic Resource Center
1-800-423-0563
http://www.wadsworth.com

For permission to use material from this text, contact us by
Web: http://www.thomsonrights.com
Fax: 1-800-730-2215
Phone: 1-800-730-2214

Printed in the United States of America
10 9 8 7 6 5 4

Preface to the Instructor

A Philosopher's Compass is intended to help students achieve a sense of how philosophical problems are motivated and what it is to formulate and address a problem philosophically. It is not a standard survey of philosophical problems, nor is it a field guide to argument forms, fallacies, and the like. There are already good books dedicated to meeting those needs. The aim of this book is to speed-up and focus the student's emerging appreciation of what it is to consider an issue in a philosophical manner. *A Philosopher's Compass* is a supplement meant to be of use to students and instructors regardless of other philosophical texts and topics studied in the course.

It is often difficult for students who are new to philosophy to sort out what is most at issue or what is the main argument or claim from all of the other things in a reading. To the instructor, there are passages that read as though they were italicized or underlined by the author, signaling key claims and moves, while the student may not have noticed them. One hope for this book is that it will accelerate student learning in that respect, giving students a heightened awareness of what to look for so that their reading, writing, and discussions are more effective.

Much of the discussion is abstract, but I try to make it accessible and illuminated with frequent illustrations and an effort to be very clear—focusing on the dimensions of issues that philosophy uniquely explores. It is very important for students to recognize the difference between being abstract and being vague, and I pay particular attention to that difference.

Chapter 1 is a discussion of how philosophical issues are motivated and how they are often grounded in quite familiar concerns and inquiries. Its aim is to express what is distinctive about philosophy while showing that it is not remote from "real" life and practical concerns.

Chapter 2 identifies some fundamental issues that are common across several different areas of philosophy. These are questions about realism and antirealism, necessity, certainty, knowledge, skepticism, and the relations between facts and values. The discussions are not meant to be compact theories but aids to identifying some of the distinctive abstract architecture of philosophy, whatever specific topic is addressed. The chapter also indicates ways in which these issues are connected. Chapter 1 gives a sense of how to begin, and Chapter 2 gives a sense of what landmarks to look for on the way.

Chapter 3 is a discussion of different philosophical methods. Descartes, for example, proceeds very differently from Aristotle or Moore. Plato and Locke go about their work in quite different ways. Here again, the aim is not to present technical information in a compact form but to describe informally some of the dramatically different conceptions of philosophical strategy, with an emphasis on starting points. One philosopher's decisive evidence is another's begged question. This chapter surveys some of the most important kinds of philosophical maneuvers by which those judgments are made.

Chapter 4 is on writing philosophy papers. It is not a "how to" chapter. It is meant to be closely connected with the previous chapters, showing their relevance to the practice of writing and vice versa. *A Philosopher's Compass* treats writing as part of the project of learning philosophy, not merely an accessory to it. This chapter illustrates some ways in which that is so.

My aspiration in writing this book has been to assist the student but not by making philosophy easier or by trying to present it in one slim volume. Rather, I hope to have discussed it in a way that will catalyze student willingness to take and to undertake philosophy seriously and to enjoy its distinctive and enduring pleasures.

Acknowledgments

I would like to thank David Tatom, Executive Editor at Harcourt College Publishers. David's grasp of what I was initially proposing with this book project, and his confidence in it, gave me the encouraging start that I needed. The Development Editor, Katie Frushour, oversaw the progress of the manuscript through several revisions. Her attention to details of expression, her suggestions concerning larger matters of the organization of the text, and her insights with regard to revising content were consistently sound, instructive, and welcome. I would also like to thank the production team, who skillfully guided my manuscript into published form: the Project Editor, Katherine Dennis; Art Director, Vicki Whistler; and Production Manager, Linda McMillan.

This text has benefited greatly from the comments by numerous reviewers, including: Elias Baumgarten, University of Michigan at Dearborn; Sherril Begres, Indiana University of Pennsylvania; Robert Burch, Texas A & M University; Robert Hollinger, Iowa State University; Lavonne Nelson, Fullerton College; Robert Sessions, Kirkwood Community College; Robert Stecker, Central Michigan University; and Jerome Wilchelns, Jefferson Community College. These reviewers made numerous, detailed comments and suggestions on drafts of the manuscript. They were constructive, thorough, and responsible. I appreciate that a great deal.

Finally, I would also like to thank my very good friend, Sandy Jeffers, for preparing the Index.

I wrote a good deal of the book during the winter and spring of 1999 while on sabbatical from my position in the Department of Philosophy and Religion at Colgate University. I spent much of that time as the John MacMurray Visiting Professor of Philosophy at the University of Edinburgh. With regard to both my home institution, and the opportunity to spend time in the department in Edinburgh, I am very fortunate and very grateful.

To my wife, Nancy, and our sons, Nathan and Daniel, I will always owe the most. This book is not about them, although they are my compass.

Preface to the Student

Some years ago when I was a graduate student, friends and I were exchanging stories at a party about things people had said to each of us when we told them that we were studying philosophy for a Ph.D. Usually this person was a stranger, someone we sat next to on an airplane or a train, for example, or perhaps it was a relative at a holiday gathering. Frequent responses were, "That's theology isn't it?" or "That's like psychology, isn't it?" Among the most humorous responses was, "Oh, what are your sayings?" Philosophers often do say things that are memorable, or deep, or interesting, but the job of the philosopher is not to think up sayings. It certainly is not what you learn to do in studying philosophy. Among other things, you learn to examine issues in depth and in ways that bring to light many aspects of them that you may not have noticed before.

The vast majority of you will be spared the awkwardness of trying to explain to a stranger just what it is a philosopher does for a living, and why you want to be one, because you will have other kinds of careers. I have tried to make *A Philosopher's Compass* an instructive book for all of you, whether you take only one course in philosophy or pursue a life-long interest in it. I hope that you will come to see that philosophy is for everyone, even those of you who may feel that it is remote from your interests. It is for everyone in respect to many of its main problems and in the way in which philosophical thought is almost unavoidable for us because we are self-aware, rational, reflective beings.

A Philosopher's Compass is meant to help you accelerate the process of recognizing what is involved in considering an issue philosophically and what is distinctive and exciting about that. It is not a "how to do philosophy" book. Given the very nature of philosophy, no book could really deliver on that promise. If what you are doing is something that can be rendered into a formula or a set of rules and techniques, then it is not philosophy. Still, there can be genuine, significant guides to finding your way on the philosophical landscape, and *A Philosopher's Compass* is meant to provide some of them.

This book is not an in-depth examination of any specific philosophical problem. *A Philosopher's Compass* is meant to help you understand important general points about philosophical problems and inquiry. Chapters 1, 2, and 3 identify and illustrate some of those points. The discussion is abstract in order to help you achieve a philosophical perspective generally, not just on this or that specific issue. Yet, the discussion is also detailed in order to bring the general features of philosophy into relief and to give you a sense of the genuineness of the issues. Chapter 4 looks at some of the aspects of writing philosophy papers because writing is such an important part of learning philosophy. An additional note on the text: Philosophers' names are in bold print and the dates of their lives are given the first time they are used. Key philosophical terms are also in bold print the first time they are used. Other terms are sometimes italicized, for the sake of emphasis. At the end of each chapter, there is a list of the philosophers mentioned in that chapter, with the dates of their lives, a list of their works that are most relevant to that chapter's discussion, and a brief note about each thinker's work. There are discussion questions at the end of each chapter, and there is a glossary at the end of the book.

A Philosopher's Compass is designed to provide clearly visible landmarks and reference points to which you can return again and again as you proceed on your journey into philosophy. The discussions of issues are intended to invite you into philosophical inquiry and to enable you to pursue it with a clear sense of what is at stake and why it is important. My hope is that *A Philosopher's Compass* will give you a start that not only tells you a bit about philosophy but motivates you to engage in it.

Contents

Chapter 1

How Did This Get Started?

IN THIS CHAPTER WE WILL LOOK AT HOW PHILOSOPHICAL problems are motivated and how they are related to experience and to other kinds of inquiry. We will also look at the crucial role of language in doing philosophy and whether philosophy makes progress.

Philosophy is different. This is not a discipline in which you will be examining a settled body of knowledge about a specific subject. Instead, you will be learning to find your way into issues that remain open and disputed. In some disciplines, such as chemistry, history, or mathematics, you study the results of inquiry that have been arrived at by experts in the field and the methods by which those results have been obtained. In these disciplines, inquiry proceeds on the basis of many things that are confidently accepted. We may continue to research and debate the causes of the French Revolution, or the effects of a certain hormone on mood, but these types of questions arise in a context of stable, shared knowledge. In philosophy, the task is to see the ways in which there are important and genuine questions that can be asked again and again. This is not because we never make progress in trying to answer them but because our understanding is always incomplete. There are always possibilities for new reflection and criticism and exploration. Philosophy involves engaging the same questions over and over again.

You will come to see how these questions can arise from your own consideration of the issues. They are not the business of only a special group of experts. As your study progresses, the ways in which philosophy is different from other disciplines will become clearer, and at the same time, philosophy will seem less remote and more relevant.

In your first philosophy course it may be a few weeks before you begin to feel that you are recognizing what is distinctive about philosophy. It can be a little while before you feel comfortable with the discipline. For one thing, it is not as though there comes a point in philosophy when you have it figured out and you can just go on in the same way. We can always go more deeply and pursue new lines of inquiry. For another, it is a discipline in which things "dawn" on us and suddenly come into view. Different things dawn on different individuals, and different things come into view at different times. You can read a work by a philosopher over and over again and continue to discover new things in it. Those new things have, in a sense, been there all along. What is different is your ability to detect claims and arguments, to make connections, and to see more deeply into the issues.

You will appreciate philosophy more and more as your comprehension and your comfort with the texts and topics increase. So, please be patient. The payoff is that before long you will experience the pleasures of finding yourself thinking and inquiring in new ways. The same things that make philosophy different and that make it difficult also make it rewarding and exciting in distinctive ways. It is not just that the problems of philosophy are interesting problems, it is exciting because of how your own thinking leads you into and through those problems.

Early on, there are some ways in which you might find this subject a bit frustrating. Perhaps you will be unconvinced that the arguments matter, or it may be unclear to you just how they are related to more familiar and concrete kinds of experience and inquiry. They *do* matter and they *are* related in ways which will come into view. *You* will bring them and their significance into view. This is not a matter of an instructor telling you what to see. In the process of doing philosophy, you find out for yourself how these arguments matter and how they are related to everyday life.

Actually, a little bit of frustration can be a good thing. It is a sign that you are beginning to grapple with new kinds of questions in new ways. Unaccustomed demands are being made on you. It is always gratifying to come to understand something, but it is even more gratifying to recognize that your intellectual perspective has been enlarged and that it is your own thinking that is most crucial to working with the issues, although you are studying the ideas and arguments of others. The point, though, is not simply to learn what others have thought but to join with them in thinking about the issues of philosophy. The payoff you will receive from patience is enormous.

What Makes Philosophy Different?

A very big part of philosophy is *making moves.* We make moves by presenting arguments, raising objections, noting conceptual connections, and crafting distinctions. These are not game-playing moves; the point is not to outwit or trick an opponent but to deepen understanding and to come closer to the truth. In aspiring to do that, philosophy is both very disciplined and unrestrained at the same time. Good moves require a high level of attention to the clarity, logic, and coherence of where you go with an issue, yet there is also a very wide scope for the imagination, speculative exploration, trying out ideas, and new formulations and insights. The discussions in chapters 2, 3, and 4 will illustrate these features of philosophy and how important they are to making moves that really advance an issue.

Philosophy makes demands upon a wide range of intellectual abilities and provides opportunities for you to contribute and to enjoy it in quite individual ways. After all, part of what makes an issue a philosophical one is that there is not some fixed "official doctrine" concerning it, in the way that, for example, the theory of elements is part of modern chemistry. As you begin to recognize moves and to make them, you will find that you are not just learning *about* a discipline, you are beginning to participate in it. You will see how these issues can be issues for you in such a way that the dialogue and the debate become actively internal to your own thoughts.

In fact, many of the issues are already your own in the sense that you have some views about them. It turns out that almost all of us have some philosophical views even if we have not studied a subject called philosophy. We all have some convictions about fundamental matters even if we have not really thought about them in a systematic way. Nearly everyone has some sort of position on whether human beings have any freedom of will, whether God exists, whether we have souls that survive the death of the body, whether anybody really has any knowledge that is certain, or whether moral judgments are ever objectively true. This does not mean that everyone's views have equal merit and plausibility. It means that much of what you do in studying philosophy is drawing out your own thinking and clarifying and reconsidering beliefs and perspectives that you already have. In that respect, even though philosophy may at first seem quite unfamiliar, it gets its starting traction in your own ideas.

Often our thinking stops at points which come too soon. Much of the time we are too sure of our beliefs and convictions. Even if our beliefs are true or could be satisfactorily justified, we frequently lack the intellectual ability to justify them. When we get into perplexities or disputes, we lack the resources to clarify and provide support for our claims.

Unfortunately, this lack of resources often leads to heated disagreements rather than joint projects of seeking the truth. We think that the person who disagrees with us is crazy, morally suspect, or not someone whose opinions we can respect. If we handle the issue philosophically, we will be able to accomplish three things. One is that we will make our own thinking more clear and effective. Another is that we will be better able to secure a hearing from those who disagree with us. The third is that we will have earned their respect. We will be able to present them with support for our claims and not just opposition.

The aim of studying philosophy is not to get you to see things a certain way but to help enhance your intellectual self-determination. There is a very great difference between having an opinion and having a view based upon justified beliefs, that is, a position *supported by reasons.* There is also a very great difference between giving an argument and just saying things. The more we are able to articulate the reasons for our beliefs, the more we can free ourselves from error, misunderstanding, and confusion.

It is to be hoped that one of the things that you will enjoy most about philosophy is appreciating the texture of issues that you thought were already settled, boring, or not of much importance. It turns out that there is plenty of room for inquiry and argument even about quite familiar matters. For example, ask yourself if it seems true that you can know something without being *certain* of it. Must you be certain in order to have genuine knowledge? And what *is* certainty? The issue of certainty and other philosophical issues are not word games. They are genuine problems that emerge quickly from reflection on many things we take for granted. For example, do you know, with certainty, that your parents did not move to a different address during the last twenty-four hours without telling you? What you will enjoy about philosophy is not so much *finding out* new things but the *activity* of rigorously examining many familiar things with your own critical understanding.

There is a sense in which philosophy is everybody's business. This is not because everyone should be a professional philosopher but because of the gain to all of us from considering things in more depth and with more discipline. Whatever philosophical issues happen to excite your interest, you will find that studying philosophy will help you to develop habits of intellectual responsibility that are completely general in their applicability. Asking "What good is philosophy?" is almost like asking "What good is disciplined thinking?" Philosophy will raise your standards of rigor, will enhance your critical skills, and will heighten your level of articulation.

The gains that come to you from meeting the demands of studying philosophy will serve you well in whatever you study or pursue. The skills you will sharpen and the new skills you will acquire in studying philosophy will help you as generalized strengths and as specialized tools. We often have the sense that there is something wrong with an argument, that there is some reason why we should not regard it as convincing. It is very valuable to be able to diagnose faulty arguments, of any type, and to be able to articulate why they are faulty. That is the sort of ability you develop in the study of philosophy.

A Case Study

We will now look at how a philosophical issue might be motivated from materials near to hand. Suppose you hear on the news that a person who has been convicted of murder has been sentenced to die. The news report also covers the views of opponents of capital punishment. They are seeking ways to reduce the sentence or at least delay the execution. There is also coverage of supporters of capital punishment who insist that nothing less than execution would be a punishment fitting the crime. This starts your thinking about the issue.

Perhaps your first thought is something like this: "What this defendant did was so awful and so unnecessary that of course he ought to be executed; he deserves it." That thought might start your wondering about just what it is that people *deserve.* What distinguishes a crime that deserves to be punished with death from one that does not? After all, many of the opponents of capital punishment shown on the news are not saying that the defendant did not commit the crime or that he should not be punished. They are saying that it is wrong and pointless to *execute* him. You still think this defendant deserves to die for his crime, but you realize that this notion of a punishment *fitting* a crime is not so straightforward. How are punishments to be fitted to crimes, and why does it seem clear to you (if it does) that execution fits murder? Does it fit *all* murders? What sort of "fit" are we talking about?

Suppose it has also been pointed out that the defendant had been living an alienated, unhappy life. He did not have stable friendships, did not hold jobs successfully, and was a binge drinker. Experts brought onto the news and talk shows explain that because of the material and emotional deprivation the defendant suffered as a child, plus the fact that his father was violent and abusive, the defendant is really not responsible for his bad character. He "never had a chance." So of course, his unhappy life spiraled out of control in this violent and regrettable way. You also listen to the prosecutor and to the police, who note that the defendant acted in a crafty and intelligent manner and not like someone who is insane or out of control. Maybe he had bad luck in his surroundings and his upbringing, but he knew what he was doing, no one made him do it, and he had the sense to try to hide his crime and cover his tracks. This offender, they conclude, is not the victim of society. He is a voluntary agent who committed a very serious crime, for which he is responsible.

As more and more coverage saturates the media, you grow tired of the whole thing. Still, after you turn off the television and after you put down the newspaper, you ask yourself, "Does he deserve *death?* Wouldn't it be enough to give him a life sentence without possibility of parole? Who knows; maybe he *is* nuts. Maybe he needs to be treated instead of punished." Then you might say to yourself something like the following; "Oh, *please;* anyone who does what he has done has no right to live. After all, what am I thinking? . . . If someone does something especially pointless and cruel, should that person be excused from responsibility because no sane person would do that? Now we have really lost our way. After all, everybody's got a story. 'My dog ate it' didn't work as an excuse for undone homework. Why should 'my father was no good' work as an excuse for murder?"

You can see that this could easily go on and on, raising questions that go deeper and wider. These are not only (or mainly) *factual* questions about this particular crime. There are, for instance, several questions here about the notion of desert. If punishment is to be deserved does this mean that the person who committed the crime must have known what he or she was doing and must have known that it was wrong? Must that person have been able to do otherwise? If any of these conditions are not met, does that undermine the notion that punishment is deserved?

Moreover, what should be the role of considerations of *desert* in justifying punishment generally? What if punishment does not seem to have much of a deterrent effect? What if it does not improve or rehabilitate those who are punished? Is it still justified because it is deserved? Should it matter whether punishment does any good? After all, isn't the fact that the person committed this serious wrongful act an adequate reason to punish him? Are there considerations other than, or in addition to, desert that could justify punishment? Why, in general *do* we punish people? Are there several different reasons?

Even if we satisfy ourselves with answers to those questions, there is yet more to think about. What should be our standards for fitting punishments to crimes? Should murdering three people be punished more severely than murdering two? What if the killer was motivated by jealous rage? Suppose he had been told lies about his victim, and they made him so angry he wanted to kill him? Is that sort of provocation a mitigating circumstance? What if the killer has no previous criminal record? Does a three-time offender deserve harsher punishment than a first-time offender?

There are many, many issues here. They are connected, but we should try to distinguish them. (1) What should be the role of desert in punishment generally? (2) What should be the role of desert in making specific determinations of the fitness of punishments to crimes? (3) What kinds of factors should count as mitigating or aggravating conditions? (4) What is the proper *aim* of punishment? (5) Must the criminal act be voluntary, and what does that mean? This is just the beginning.

How seriously should we take the defendant's misfortune with respect to his upbringing? He had terrible role models. He was not encouraged to do well in school and to act responsibly. He grew up in a setting where disagreements were handled by threats and force. What chance did he have to develop a decent character? Nevertheless, shouldn't he be able to control himself from going so far as to commit murder? Plenty of people experience similar misfortune and do not commit serious crimes. If we are willing to explain away his responsibility, should we explain away the responsibility of the person with excellent character who does excellent things? Are we going to say that *that* person's character is the product of factors and influences over which he or she had no control? When people do things that we admire or for which we are grateful, do we think that acting in that way is unavoidable for them and that they do not deserve credit for acting in ways they could not help?

These questions about the extent to which individuals are responsible for their characters and about the nature of voluntary action are connected with questions about what is reasonable to expect of people.

They are connected with our views about what people can and cannot help doing. How often is it really true when someone says, "I couldn't help it"? Trying to resolve one of these issues by itself is bound to fail because of the connections between them. It is like trying to flatten a waterbed. The bulges keep coming up, and they do so in a lot of different places.

Much depends upon whether the act was voluntary and deliberate. So, we need to arrive at some confident judgments about the accused person's state of mind at the time of committing the crime. How do we know whether the agent fully understood what he was doing? Could it not be the case that an agent acts knowingly and willingly but is still unavoidably caused to act in that way by causal factors operating on him? Is causal determinism (the claim that all of our actions are necessitated by preceding events) compatible with moral responsibility? What if the act was wildly out of character for this man? Is that evidence that he was somehow less in control of himself and that his responsibility for the act should be diminished?

Another factor that can be quite important is *time.* Suppose the person who committed the crime is only caught and convicted seventeen years after the crime. Should that matter? He might argue that he has lived a responsible and decent life since then, that he is a changed man and no longer the same person as the murderer. One response to this is that if he is guilty, then he should be punished; it does not matter what time it is. Another response is that it does matter what time it is because it matters how the guilty person has used the time. Suppose he is genuinely repentant. Should that count against a severe sentence? If the change in character is genuine and substantial, should we punish the person who is before us *now,* after the change? There are hard and important moral issues here, and they are intricately connected with hard and important questions about personal identity, responsibility for character, and continuity of character.

By now, our issues have expanded to range over several matters in addition to the issue of punishment. The following are just some of them:

1. the nature of responsibility and voluntary action;
2. how to sort out factors that are influences on people from factors that causally determine their actions;
3. how we can have knowledge of other persons' states of mind;
4. the relation of one's state of mind to responsibility; and

5. the relation of the rationale for punishment to the continuity or discontinuity of a person's character.

The claims that we make about any one of them have implications for the others.

The upshot is something that can be discovered again and again. What may initially look like a fairly straightforward, stand-alone matter, is actually part of a large, complex system of issues, the components of which are in complex relations of explanation and justification.

Facts and Philosophy

It is important to notice that it is not just one or the other of the issues in the list that is *the* philosophical issue. Rather, the philosophical dimension of an issue often concerns the ways in which genuine questions about it remain even though there are not straightforward factual answers to these questions. Questions such as, "In what respects should punishment be based upon what people deserve?" or "What are the differences between influences on character and determinants of it?" are philosophical in nature. We are not saying that the facts are not important; of course they are. There are, though, important disputes about what the facts *count for,* and those disputes often have a philosophical dimension.

Suppose that there is no doubt that the convicted defendant committed the murder. That is a fact. Suppose that there is no doubt that he sought to escape the authorities and that he exhibited some real cunning in doing so. Suppose that he has a record including disorderly conduct, petty larceny, and loitering. None of these (and large numbers of other facts) on their own or together settles the issues we raised above. We will see as our discussion proceeds that this is generally true of philosophical issues. Reflection on experience and factual matters can raise the deepest philosophical issues. Philosophical thinking is needed to address them.

One timely issue in which there is an important role for the facts, but which the facts do not resolve, is the issue of affirmative action. There are facts about the differences in annual income between different racial groups and between men and women. We can gather information about the representation of different groups in different occupations. There is data about the admission to colleges and universities of members of various groups, and so forth. Much of the controversy about policies of affirmative action concerns what these facts show. They might indicate that there has been significant progress in income gains for certain groups, yet the facts alone do not decide the issue of how fast progress should be made to satisfy reasonable standards of fairness.

The affirmative action debate is an excellent example of how several different *kinds* of issues are often interconnected, and philosophical inquiry is an especially effective way to identify them. There are complex debates about why certain groups are so little represented in particular occupations. Is this because of discrimination, or is it for other reasons? (That is a *causal* question.) Is giving preference to members of groups that have suffered discrimination itself a kind of unfairness? (That is an *ethical* question.) We need to sort out just what affirmative action *is.* Is it a set of policies to eliminate barriers and types of exclusion, is it a strategy of compensation, or is it a program to achieve certain levels of representation by certain groups? (That is a *conceptual* question.)

Countless familiar issues have equally real philosophical dimensions, and we will present some additional illustrations of how philosophical questions can be easily motivated by reflection on facts. These examples do not involve the sorts of urgent ethical questions raised by capital punishment and affirmative action, yet they are equally complex and significant.

Suppose we want to know why two dozen students became ill after lunch. They all ate in the university dining hall, and they ate a variety of different things. So, it looks like it was not just the fish, the salad dressing, the pie, or any particular food item alone. We eventually find the cause of the illness. It was bacteria on some of the serving utensils. This is a causal explanation that could be made much more detailed. The health inspectors and operators of the food service will gather all the facts they can, but there are also matters of philosophical importance for us to notice.

First, observe the close connection between the notions of explanation and causation. Many explanations are causal explanations. When we want to understand something we often look for its cause. Being told "Oh, it just happened, that's all" is no explanation. Also, a thorough causal explanation, one that is really illuminating, often goes beneath the surface. There are experts on food-related illnesses and on bacteria and so forth. Just saying "It was food poisoning" is not precise enough for many purposes. The move from everyday explanations to scientific explanations involves an increase in precision and detail.

A scientific explanation of why the students became ill, why a plane crashed, or why there was a particularly wet winter in a certain part of the world, typically involves trying to identify the laws of nature that govern those sorts of things. Everyone knows that diet and exercise are important factors with respect to heart disease, but there is an important difference between that informal, almost commonsensical awareness and a scientific understanding of the actual causal processes at work. Now, we might wonder what could there be for philosophy to do that successful science cannot do? Is there some special sort of concern that philosophy addresses that science does not?

The answer to that question is yes, but that is not because there is some way in which science fails. It is because no matter how advanced they are, scientific practices and theories themselves raise distinctively philosophical questions. (In using the term "science" in this context, I do not mean just physics, chemistry, and biology. I mean any systematic, organized inquiry that seeks to explain certain sorts of things. So of course economics, anthropology, psychology, and some other disciplines are to be counted as sciences.) A large part of science is searching for causal explanations, but the issue of what causality is, is a philosophical question.

We might say things such as "a cause is what makes something happen" or "a cause brings something about," but once we start asking what distinguishes a causal relation from other relations, we find that we are engaged in philosophical reflection. Does smoking cause cancer? Does advertising tobacco products cause people to smoke? Does use of tobacco products cause addiction to nicotine? A great deal hangs on the way we understand causality. Are all human actions caused, or is there some sense in which we have freedom of will and can act without being caused to do so? For example, if we think that advertising influences but does not determine behavior, we are making an important point about causation. (It is a point similar to one we made above about the influences on a person's character.) The distinction between what influences character and what determines it is one that is directly relevant to each of us. It is also an excellent example of how important a philosophical issue can be. After all, our concern is not just whether smokers or tobacco companies are responsible, but with the nature of free agency and also what sort of self-understanding we have.

When we are philosophically engaged with an issue, we should not leave the facts behind. Analysis and reflection help us to interpret the facts, and the facts keep us tethered to the genuine, specific issues that raised the philosophical question in the first place. Even the sciences always have a philosophical dimension, although in the ordinary practice of science, philosophical questions are not raised. In science, we want to know at what temperature this metal melts, how far away that star is, or whether this drug will suppress an immunological response, and so forth; yet the issues of what makes for a good explanation and what is the difference between a law of nature and an accidental generalization are philosophical issues. Science can help clarify what the philosophical issues are, but it does not solve them.

This holds for both the natural sciences and the social sciences. For example, social scientists often study the moral beliefs of communities, age-groups, societies, and whole cultures. There are comparative studies, historical studies, studies of different economic groups, different religious groups, etc. While all of these are important parts of the overall science of human nature and social life, we should see if anything remains for distinctively *philosophical* consideration.

Let's consider morality. There are several different views about the source of moral beliefs. Perhaps you hold that morality is a subjective matter in the sense that moral values are based on feelings and attitudes. You might instead hold that there are objective answers to moral questions and that *of course* some views are objectively correct and others are objectively mistaken. Maybe you maintain that morality has a basis in religion. Also, many people maintain that our morals are based on social or cultural norms that we internalize as a result of growing up and living in a certain environment. There are some plausible reasons in favor of each of these views. Yet, they cannot all be true.

Let's suppose that a version of the last one is basically right and that there are quite good causal explanations for people's moral beliefs. Let's also suppose that these explanations show how values are transmitted from generation to generation and how group cohesion and cultural identity are reinforced by shared moral norms. This approach explains moral beliefs in terms of social psychology and the function of shared values. We can account for moral beliefs and practices in terms of history, culture, and the phenomena of social life that can be scientifically investigated.

To insist that there remains a task for philosophy is not to say that social scientific explanations are flawed or incomplete. They may be excellent as *social scientific explanations.* Still, there are genuine questions about moral values that are philosophical questions, questions that are *not* finally and conclusively settled by the various sciences. These are questions of justification and the strength of reasons for one moral view as opposed to another. The fact that people have certain moral beliefs and that there is a causal explanation of how they came to have them leaves plenty of room for a critical examination of those beliefs and a determination of whether they are sound or not. A social scientific explanation may give a detailed and illuminating account of the moral views that sustained the institution of slavery in the American South. The question of whether there are reasons that adequately justify the institution is another matter. The *source* of a view and the grounds for it may be quite different. Moral philosophy should not ignore facts about society and psychology. It does though, have its own issues, which are raised by reflection on those facts.

The Importance of Language

Philosophical issues are raised by many kinds of inquiry and experience, and you will find that getting control of the language of philosophy is a large part of gaining control over philosophical issues. The precision and clarity of our use of language is intimately connected with the precision and clarity of our thought. They can reinforce each other, or they can undermine each other. Sometimes terms are used in unfamiliar ways. Sometimes they are just plain unfamiliar terms. Do not let your confusion about what terms mean go without inquiry. It is rare that a philosophical debate is just *semantic* and that it is no more than a disagreement about the use of terms. Nonetheless, semantic issues are very important. After all, we use words to talk about the world (and about God and numbers and everything else), so *clarity about the use of terms enhances clarity about the subject of the discussion.*

Consider, for example, the word "person." It is important in several areas of philosophy. It is a key term in moral theorizing (What sorts of attitudes and duties are owed to persons in contrast to non-persons?); in arguments about personal identity (What makes me the *same* person through time and change?); and in the debate about free will and determinism (Persons, unlike other creatures, are often thought to possess will and to act freely. What *is* a free will, and is there such a thing?) It can also figure in arguments about the nature of mind and body, immortality, and even in topics of political philosophy (topics such as the basis and scope of rights, liberties, and protections). Everybody uses the word, but when you stop to consider just what it means, you see that there is need for careful analysis.

We can see this when we consider the relations between the meaning of the term "person" and the biological classification *Homo sapiens.* Does, or should, the meaning of the term "person" depend upon our scientific understanding of the biology of human nature? Does one's identity as a person over time depend upon psychological considerations, or physical ones, or both? Could there be individuals who are persons but not human beings? These are not just questions about the use of a word. When we raise these questions about the word, we are raising questions about the concept of a person and about what a person is. Also, we see again an illustration of our earlier points about the connection between philosophical issues.

Often someone will insist that key terms be defined. Certainly clarity concerning how terms are being used is crucial, yet in philosophy you will often find that definitions cannot be put forward right at the start. Sometimes definitions are a result of the discussion. We may need to find out how to define terms by examining the issues to which they are important. Consider "person" again. We need to think about the various contexts in which it is used and the various ways it is used in those contexts before a clear sense of its meaning can be articulated. You may believe that persons are owed certain kinds of regard and treatment that are not owed to non-persons. You may believe that only persons have moral rights. You might wonder if persons are all of the same kind. For example, if God exists, is God a person? Does the term apply to God in the same way it applies to us?

Many terms invite this kind of careful consideration, and many, if not most, terms have more than one meaning. There is an important difference between a term having a *clear* meaning and a *single* meaning. A term may have several clear meanings. Ask yourself what is the meaning of the word "responsible" or "alive" or "good" or "cause." Compare the meaning of "cause" in the following three statements.

1. The cause of William and Angela's divorce was William's infidelity.
2. The loose bolt was the cause of the engine falling from the wing of the airplane.
3. The rise in inflation was the cause of the higher prices and the unrest among the factory workers.

In each usage the meaning may be clear, but there may be somewhat different meanings (or kinds of causality) in the different usages. Supplying someone with a motive (William's infidelity is why Angela wants a divorce) may not be causation in exactly the same sense as in the airplane's loss of an engine.

We often find that we can use a term quite fluently even if it turns out to be very difficult to give a single, fixed definition of it. We all agree that it is wrong to cause other people pain just for fun, but there is plenty of philosophical work to be done in achieving a satisfactory account of the meaning of "wrong." You might find that you agree with others to a very large extent about what is right and what is wrong but at the same time disagree about the meaning of the terms "right" and "wrong." You may agree that "wrong" means "should not be done" or "merits condemnation," but you give very different renderings of *why.* You give different interpretations of the basis for thinking those things. (We shall say a bit about some of those interpretations in chapter 2.)

Consider another example. You would probably insist that you know what a tiger is and that you can quite reliably recognize tigers. You have no trouble distinguishing them from lions, pythons, antelopes, and other animals, but what is the definition of "tiger"? What *should* it be? Any number of perfectly familiar terms could be used to run the same test.

There are important philosophical questions raised by these observations:

1. In order to use a term meaningfully must one be able to give its definition?
2. How are we to distinguish between what belongs to the meaning of a term and what does not? (Tigers are carnivorous. They also sleep a lot, and their numbers are declining. Are these parts of the meaning of the word "tiger"?)
3. In what ways are the various meanings of a term related?
4. What is it that you understand when you understand the meaning of a term?

These are questions which indicate how issues of definition are related to questions about the nature of knowledge, the relations between concepts and language, and the relations between language and the world.

The philosophical exploration of an issue often requires very careful attention to language. Looking in a dictionary can be of some help. Dictionaries are good resources for finding out about contemporary usage and getting some idea of the multiple meanings of words. Also, some dictionaries supply information about the history of terms. They may tell us when they were first used, how their meanings have changed, and so on. A dictionary, however, cannot be used to settle philosophical disputes.

The ordinary use of a term may not be adequately precise for its use in philosophy. A philosopher of science may want a very exact and detailed account of just what is a *theory* or just what constitutes an *explanation.* An ethical theorist may want a very precise understanding of just what is the difference between a *natural* right and a *civil* right. Someone reflecting on the nature of knowledge may aim at supplying a rigorous account of *certainty* and just what conditions must be fulfilled in order for a claim to be certain. A dictionary can provide important information and reminders, but it cannot do philosophical work for us. Clarity and precision in the use of the language of philosophy are crucial *because* the issues are not merely verbal. They are substantive issues, and language is our access to them.

What Is Philosophical Progress?

Many philosophical issues are centuries old and many philosophers still regarded as great are figures from antiquity and the middle ages. This might lead you to wonder whether philosophers ever get anywhere. How advanced can a discipline be if some of its current "heroes" are over two thousand years old?

The great philosophers are the ones who had especially profound insights and formulated arguments that still command our respect. Their importance and their influence endure because what they took to be the fundamental issues really are fundamental issues. They arise in new forms and are motivated by the concerns and issues of our lives in our time, but they are issues that a reflective person in any time finds almost unavoidable. Again, whatever the state of the special sciences, whatever the state of technological development, there are philosophical questions about knowledge, value, rationality, and other fundamental matters. The great philosophers succeeded in formulating and addressing those questions in ways that continue to be fruitful.

Has there been progress, or are the debates about these issues just endless and inconclusive? There has been progress in the sense that ambiguities are removed, errors in reasoning are exposed, constant adjustments to advances in factual knowledge are made, and so forth. What makes a contribution to philosophy important is not that it is correct once and for all, but that it contains resources we can continually employ and develop in our own thinking. It is not as though there are answers to philosophical questions "out there" and the great philosophers are the ones who show us what they are. Rather, they give us ideas, distinctions, and arguments, and they show us possibilities that are inexhaustibly relevant.

This is illustrated by the works of say, **Aristotle** (384–322 B.C.) or **John Locke** (1632–1704), two thinkers from distant ages whose works continue to have influence on even the most contemporary philosophy.[1] (In chapters 2 and 3 we will discuss some of the ways in which this is true.) Each of them makes several claims about the nature of the physical world and about the mechanisms of perception and other matters that the special sciences (such as physics, chemistry, physiology, neuroscience, and so forth) address today. What Aristotle and Locke wrote may sound quaint, unsophisticated, and just plain wrong, but when you read a philosophical text, you are not reading it to acquire factual information. You are reading it to develop more subtle and illuminating ways of understanding enduring questions and problems. Aristotle's and Locke's views about such things as the general features of knowledge and about the relation of thought to objects are still of the first importance, even if the state of the sciences in their day was what we would now regard as backward.

There is no doubt that we now have a much larger and more detailed understanding of physical and chemical properties and processes than these philosophers had. Still, there remains the difficult philosophical question of what account we should give of say, "What is an object?" That may sound like a very odd question, but it is a concern that can be expressed by other questions that do not sound nearly so odd. Consider the following:

1. Under what conditions is something the *same* even though it has changed? (Think about a plant that has grown, or a machine with its parts replaced, or a patient who has become irreversibly comatose.)
2. Is an object nothing but a collection of qualities, or is it something distinct from the qualities which it has? (Think about a table, its shape, the material it is made of, its color, and so forth.)
3. Is there a difference between qualities which an object *must* have in order to be that object and those which it might lack and still be *that* object? (Consider, for example, whether something which is a human being could be a human being even if it were not a mammal. If you answer "No, that's impossible!" what sort of impossibility is that?)
4. Are there real and distinct kinds of things independent of our beliefs, concepts, and perceptions? Do our concepts and ways of classifying objects shape the order of things in the world? (Are there *really* quarks and electrons and genes, or are these

just useful theoretical fictions? Are there *really* tables and human beings or *really* just quarks and electrons and genes?)

It is in regard to questions like these that thinkers such as Aristotle and Locke still have very important things to say to us. The body of our scientific knowledge is much larger than in the past, as well as more accurate and more explanatory. We can do much better at explaining the food poisoning incident than inquirers could have in Locke's or Aristotle's time. However, natural science has not eliminated the philosophical dimensions of fundamental questions about the world and knowledge, including scientific knowledge.

The main reason that philosophical debates go on and on is not because they lead nowhere but because philosophy is thinking that is relentless. There is always a fuller understanding that is possible. There are always new connections to make and new objections to which we can respond. A philosophical position is not a set of fixed, final answers to fixed questions. It is a way of seeing what the questions are and a way of seeing what kinds of considerations can help us to answer them. There is always more to see and there are always new ways to look. You should see your study of philosophy not only as an examination of a number of specific texts and topics, but also, and perhaps primarily, as a way of challenging and enlarging your intellectual abilities overall and your own awareness of what you are able to do with them. That is philosophical progress.

Where We Are Now

Let's review what we have found so far.

1. Philosophical questions are not difficult to motivate. There are several persistent, fundamental problems of philosophy, but we can formulate many of them just by reflecting on our experience and our understanding of ourselves and the world.
2. A single philosophical question or concern is very likely to be connected with many others. Philosophical issues cannot be rigidly compartmentalized because what we think about one of them has implications for what we think about others. Much of philosophical thinking is tracing out these implications, seeing where they lead, and making careful judgments about whether to revise our starting points in light of what they lead to.

3. The questions which are generated in philosophy are not the sorts of questions that are addressed directly by the sciences. Working on them often requires paying close attention to the facts, but the facts on their own do not resolve the issues. The kinds of questions that we raise in thinking philosophically are questions that require philosophical answers. There is rigorous thinking about important issues that is not confined to the boundaries or methods of any of the sciences.
4. Special and constant attention is to be paid to language. The usefulness and success of distinctions, objections, arguments, and illustrations depend upon clear articulation.

It is true that we can study the French Revolution without also going into philosophical depth about the nature of justice or political legitimacy, and we can study the human genome in very fine detail without going into questions about the value of a human life. That should not mislead us into thinking that maybe philosophy really is not very important, that it is subjective opinion, or that it is detached from concrete concerns and from the things that "really" matter. Engaging in philosophical thinking is not turning our attention away from the genuine concerns of experience and inquiry. It is looking beneath their surface to try to discover the assumptions that we make and the conclusions that we draw and to critically examine them. It is also to acknowledge that many ideas and beliefs which we ordinarily regard as unproblematic really are problematic.

Also, it is not only in the sciences or in the moral context that we find the resources and the opportunities to motivate philosophical issues. Another very rich source is literature. This is true of countless novels, stories, and plays from antiquity to the present. As your study of philosophy progresses, you will begin to notice just how philosophical the issues are that many writers write about. The ways in which these works connect with us is often a matter of the ways in which they raise deep and difficult questions about the nature of desire, self-knowledge, what we owe to others, personal identity, and the meaning of life. For example, Joseph Conrad's *Lord Jim* raises deep and difficult issues about conscience, the role of the past in a person's self-conception, and the nature of self-realization. In quite different, but also very compelling ways, Toni Morrison's *Beloved* raises some of those same issues and also different issues about fundamental human needs and about the nature of love and friendship. In Shakespeare's *Hamlet*, *The Immoralist* by Gide, *The Stranger* by Camus, or *Crime and Punishment* by Dostoevsky, you find some of the fundamental issues of philosophy embodied in the characters and in their actions. Perhaps before, philosophy seemed remote and unconnected to real life. You should now be able to see that opportunities for it are everywhere.

After philosophically examining an issue, we may find ourselves still holding on to the beliefs with which we started—yet, the way in which we hold them is different. We now have reasoned convictions that we can defend. If we disagree with someone, we can now give grounds for our position, and we have the resources to respond to objections. This is a way in which philosophy is everyone's business. It is everyone's business to be intellectually responsible, to have reasons for his or her views, and to be able to meet challenges to them.

In addition, we can no more just *do* philosophy without being motivated by some specific question or concern, than we can just *try,* without trying to do some specific thing. If you ask someone what she is doing and she says, "Oh, nothing in particular; I'm just trying," the response makes no sense. Maybe there is some further explanation. Maybe she is trying to clear her mind of distractions and trying to put aside numerous worries, or maybe she is working up her resolve to do something she knows will be difficult. There is no such thing as just *trying.* Similarly, philosophical thinking always has some object, some guiding concern, even if it is something very general such as "the meaning of life" or "the possibility of objective knowledge."

To be sure, a good deal of philosophy is about issues that are fundamental and often abstract: Are there objective values? Can the existence of God be proven? What is the relation of mind to body? Is there such a thing as Free Will? What are the conditions which must be met by knowledge-claims? Yet it is not only those large and deep questions that comprise the business of philosophy. They are important parts of it because of how they relate to so many other, more familiar things. There is plenty of philosophy to do regarding assisted suicide, pornography, the prohibition of smoking in public places, the portrayal of violence in movies and video games, and so forth. As you examine these issues critically and move beyond what seems obvious initially, you find yourself raising questions about the nature of self-determination, the notion of what is a good life, and the basic principles of a just society. You also find that thinking philosophically matters much more than perhaps you initially thought and that it applies to many more areas.

The ways in which philosophical thought is abstract enable us to better understand familiar, concrete matters. Sometimes a high level of abstraction is needed to illuminate and explain what is concrete, real, and right there with us in our lives. Abstractions don't always distance us from the object of inquiry. They can be instrumental in focusing our thought on fundamentals. In the next chapter, we will show how by looking at some of the general features of philosophical problems and beginning to map the philosophical landscape.

Some Things to Think About and Discuss

1. Should statements from the victim about how the crime has affected the victim and his or her family and loved ones be allowed to influence sentencing? Suppose the person being sentenced has already been convicted of other crimes. Should that person's record influence the sentence for this crime?
2. Are you the same person you were five years ago? What criteria do you use to answer that question? What is the relation between personal identity and continuity of character? Does it seem to you that character, personality, and personal identity are three different things? What are the differences between them?
3. How do you understand the relation between acting freely and doing what you want to do? Are those the same? If not, what is the difference between them? Could a person be free to do what he wants but still lack freedom of the will? If there are thirty-five brands of breakfast cereal in one store and only twenty in another, do you have more freedom when you shop in the first store because there are more choices? Is the number of options the key to freedom?

Key Philosophers and Texts

Aristotle (384–322 B.C.) *Metaphysics, Physics:* In these works, Aristotle develops his theories of substance, essence, and change. In addition to their importance in the history of philosophy, Aristotle's arguments and distinctions are still important to philosophical debates about how something remains the same entity during change and how entities are to be classified as members of the same kind.

John Locke (1632–1704) *An Essay Concerning Human Understanding:* A classic of British Empiricism, presenting a crucial view of the presuppositions and the implications of early modern science. This work set much of the philosophical agenda for philosophers after Locke.

Endnote

1. These are the only two philosophers mentioned by name in this chapter. Some of their views will be more fully discussed in what follows. Also, many other philosophers will be mentioned, and all of the philosophers and texts discussed in chapters 2, 3, and 4 are as relevant to chapter 1 as are Aristotle and Locke. You will see why as we proceed.

Chapter 2

What Makes It Philosophy?

WE WILL CONTINUE TO DEVELOP OUR DISCUSSION OF WHAT is distinctive about philosophy. In particular, we will identify some of the most general contours of philosophical positions and the ways in which those contours are common to very different contexts of inquiry. We also will explore some of the connections between philosophical positions.

We saw in chapter 1 that there are philosophical dimensions to many issues that we do not ordinarily think of as philosophical. There are always questions of conceptual clarification, and there are assumptions and implications that need to be brought to light. It turns out that there are connections between seemingly unrelated topics that are all part of what is involved in looking at something philosophically. An issue such as capital punishment, for example, is related to questions about freedom of will, the principles of justice, and the justification and aims of punishment generally. In this chapter, we bring into view some important abstract features *shared* by *different* philosophical problems. The value of doing this is that it will bring into relief some of the most basic, abstract contours of philosophical topics and inquiry. Our aim is not to explore these issues in depth but to identify some of the abstract contours they share. That will help give you a clearer perspective on how certain distinctive philosophical questions are common to many different contexts.

The Point of Abstraction

Philosophical thought works extensively with abstractions, and we should say something about the way in which abstract thinking is important in philosophy. Perhaps you have heard people (including yourself) say things such as, "Philosophy is just a lot of abstractions," or, "Philosophy sounds interesting, but I really want to study something concrete and more connected to real life." It *is* true that in philosophical inquiry we often engage in quite abstract thought.

Being abstract, though, does not mean being unconnected with experience and the world of real things. For example, think of your best friend. You can think of that person very concretely, as a unique individual distinct from everyone and everything else. You can also think of your friend as someone roughly your age, as a mammal, as an animal, as a living thing, and so forth. Each of these ways of thinking of that person involves abstraction. Each leaves something out and considers the individual in a certain determinate way. Another example of abstraction is this: Think of the way an individual organism is classified as a member of a species, a genus, a family, an order, a class, and a phylum. That is a series of increasing abstraction. Thought of *all* kinds (not just classifying plants and animals) involves abstraction. When you are trying to figure out what gift to give someone, you might think, "I'll get her that new biography of Queen Elizabeth because she loves biographies." You are employing abstractions. The concept *biography* is more abstract than the concept *biography of Queen Elizabeth,* and the concept *book* is more abstract than the concept *biography.* Indeed, we use abstractions all the time, and we are more familiar with them than we might think.

However, being abstract and being vague are different. When abstract considerations are also vague it is because they have not been formulated effectively. Abstract reasoning can and should be very precise and very clear. One place in which this is easily illustrated is in diagnosing the structure of an argument. When you formalize an argument, showing just its logical structure and not worrying about the particular subject matter, that is a clear case of abstract thinking. For example, consider the following argument: If it is raining, then the game will be canceled. The game will be canceled. Therefore, it is raining. The abstract form of the argument is this:

(Premise 1) If X then Y.
(Premise 2) Y.
(Conclusion) Therefore X.

Look over the argument and the argument form. There are any number of arguments that share the same form. They could be arguments about anything. If any argument of that form is **valid** (or is **invalid**) then *every* argument of that form is valid (or invalid). An argument has a **logical form**, which specifies the relations between its components. To be valid, the conclusion must follow from the premises as a logical consequence of them. It is not a question of what the statements in the argument are about or what language they are written in. What matters with respect to validity is logical form and that is an abstract matter which is quite exact.

Does the sample argument (and its form) seem to you to be valid or invalid? In fact, the argument is invalid, and every argument that has the same form is invalid and involves the same basic **fallacy**. (A fallacy is an error in reasoning.) Can you think of a way to explain *why* it is invalid? This is exactly the sort of issue a logic course pursues very systematically. We will not undertake a full-fledged discussion of logical form here. For our purposes, logical form is relevant as a vivid illustration of the way in which what is abstract can also be very exact and clear. To think abstractly is to leave things out, but leaving things out in the right sorts of ways can also bring very important things into view.

Often in philosophy we want to be able to make points with highly general significance. For example, we might want to make a point about the nature of emotions and not just about some specific emotion such as anger, envy, or gratitude. We might want to do this if we are interested in some general connections between emotions and beliefs, for example. Does each emotion have a belief as a component? For instance, if you feel grateful, does that require that you believe that someone has done something for you that merits your appreciation? Are emotions utterly different in kind from beliefs? Or, we might want to make a point about artifacts generally, in contrast to naturally occurring things; after all, money does not grow on trees. We may also want to characterize artifacts as a single huge class of things rather than talking about specific kinds of them such as frying pans, battleships, gummy bears, or sweaters.

As you proceed in your study of philosophy, you will begin to notice that there are certain general concerns that come up again and again in different problem areas. In addition to the specific issues and the disputes about these concerns, there is a *general abstract architecture* that you may begin to notice, and this cuts across the boundaries of those disputes and topics. In the remainder of this chapter, we will identify and illustrate some of these general concerns and how they structure philosophical problems. The topics that are selected to illustrate these concerns are important topics, but the main focus is on the abstract issues that they illustrate.

Causation and Morality: The Common Contours of Different Landscapes

Let's start by noticing something familiar. Our thinking is richly supplied with what we might call *causal* concepts, and our language is richly supplied with *causal* terms, such as "break," "frighten," "freeze," "excite," "burn," "infect," and a huge number of others. (You should be able to think of dozens of them.) These are all different ways in which things happen or are *caused*. The way in which we think about and understand the world depends very substantially on causal concepts.

The notion of causation may seem to be an unexciting one, but it has been selected as an illustration because it is extremely important. Causal thinking plays a key role in holding together our conception of the world. It is fundamental to our conception of how the world works. For example, when you see a neat circle of stones in a clearing in the forest, you conclude that people have been there because you know that it is very improbable that the stones just formed a circle without people arranging them that way. That is causal thinking. On the basis of what you are perceiving now (looking at the stones arranged into what you recognize as a fireplace) you make an inference about how they got into that arrangement. Another example is when you lunge to catch an egg rolling off a counter in the kitchen. You believe that the egg striking the floor after falling will cause the uncooked egg to splatter and make a mess. This is causal thinking. It is also causal thinking that is behind your decision to take an aspirin when you have a headache and to give vitamins to your five-year-old child. If the child asks, "Why do I have to take these?" and you answer, "Because they are good for you; they help you stay healthy and strong," you are giving an answer in terms of the causal properties of vitamins. Causal thinking is everywhere, and a great deal of it we simply take for granted. It is so much a part of our experience that it can seem almost as though we know without giving any thought to it—that ice will melt if heated, that being burned is painful, and countless other things.

It is plain that there is a large family of causal concepts and that we use them all the time. We will see where this is leading in a moment. First, we need to take a look at one other important group of concepts.

There is a large set of *moral* concepts and *moral* terms, such as "dishonest," "unfair," "cruel," "deceitful," "cowardly," etc. These are all concepts of how an act, practice, or characteristic can be morally wrong. This is analogous to how the terms mentioned above indicate ways in which a process or an activity can be *causal.* (Of course, there are many concepts and terms referring to morally *good* acts and characteristics, but we will just use concepts of what is wrong to simplify the illustration.) We may not always use the word "cause" when we are thinking in causal terms, and we may not always use the word "wrong" when we are thinking of ways in which something is morally unacceptable. Still, one large, familiar family of concepts is connected through the notion of causation, and this other large, familiar family of concepts is connected through the notion of moral wrongness. We are now able to move on from the quite concrete to the more abstract, in order to make a central point about philosophy.

Consider a familiar causal process, such as freezing. Now, when we see that something has frozen, we may observe changes in it (let's just imagine that it is a quantity of water), but we do not also see some additional thing we call "causality." We see, for example, the water and then the ice but not the causality. Another example might be when we throw a piece of chalk on the floor, we see it strike the floor and shatter, but we do not also observe some additional thing, namely, causality. The point is not that there might be something fictional or mysterious about causality. The point is that we need to examine and interpret the notion of causality in order to understand *how it applies to the world.* It is not difficult to give examples of causality, but "seeing" causality is not just like seeing an elephant, a grilled cheese sandwich, or your desk. Before we pursue this matter, we will take a moment to notice something very similar about the notion of being morally wrong.

When we see someone (without provocation) savagely attack another person who the attacker knows is innocent, we see the attack and the suffering of the victim, but the wrongness of it is not some additional thing that we perceive. There are some good, clear reasons why this is a wrong thing to do. We might say that what the assailant did was wrong because (a) it was a deliberate attack on an innocent person, (b) it was a use of excessive force, (c) it caused unnecessary harm and pain, (d) it was done in a spirit of cruelty, or (e) it was unprovoked. However, in our present discussion, the issue is not, "Why is it wrong to beat innocent people?" We *know* why we think the action is wrong. The issue here is, "How does the concept *wrong* (or any moral concept) apply to acts?" In other words, is the wrongness (or the goodness or the rightness) of the act an *objective* feature of it? What could that mean? If it is not, what could *that* mean? Our philosophical concern is, "What is the best account of how the concept wrong applies to anything?" What should be coming into view is that *this is the same abstract concern we had about causality.*

These examples show that even a quick consideration of some of the most familiar concepts reveal important questions about the relation of thought to the world. What may seem surprising is that the questions we can raise about the concept *causality* are very similar to the questions we can raise about the concept *wrong.* Some of the most general and important philosophical questions are the same questions in different contexts. This is the sort of abstract architecture we need to recognize and become comfortable with.

Answers to questions about what causes something are arrived at in scientific inquiry or in ordinary experience. (What caused the engine to fail? Why did Aunt Jean break out in hives? Why did the shirt shrink so much?) Similarly, questions about what is right and wrong are questions for moral theory and for careful reflection for all of us. (Is it ever permissible to make a deceitful promise? Do we have any responsibility to future generations? Is it permissible to punish someone in order to deter others?) Often, there are arguments about whether we have answered our causal questions or moral questions correctly. Is that really the cause? Are those adequate reasons for thinking that actions of that type should be morally prohibited? There is also another level at which these issues can be examined, and this is the level we are moving to now. At this other level, the issues have the *same general form.* When we look at the issues at this abstract level the concern is not about what causes something, or whether such and such is wrong and why; it is a concern about how to understand the relation of a concept to the world. We think with concepts, but we think *about* the world. How are the two related? Now we are doing philosophy.

Realism and Antirealism: The Relation of Concept to Object

We are heading for a quite high level of abstraction, but the issue is one that is not foreign to you. We can illustrate the relation between the abstract and the concrete in the following way. We often find ourselves arguing about whether claims of some specific sort are objective. Sometimes people will say things along these lines: "Science is objective, but morality is subjective." "Taste in art is subjective."

"Many people think that science gives a true view of reality, but it is really just a cultural construct. It is not objectively true." Arguments about what is subjective and what is objective occur quite frequently outside of philosophy. Often these are arguments about whether our beliefs, concepts, and theories "tell it like it is" and report how the world is or whether how we take the world to be *depends* in some fundamental way on our beliefs, concepts, and theories. That is one way of formulating the issue we have motivated—by talking about causality and morality.

It is very likely that you already have a basic stand on this issue, though thinking about it in just this way may be new. Perhaps you hold that causality (or wrongness, beauty, or whatever it is that is in question) is a *real* feature of the world *independent* of how we think about it or perceive it. You would then argue that the correct way to interpret causality is in terms of it being a *real* relation between things in the world. You would argue that whether an act is morally right or wrong is not a matter of how we feel about it or a matter of cultural norms. You would argue that the act is right or wrong because of what *it* is. Or, perhaps your view is that causality (or wrongness, beauty, or whatever is in dispute) is *not* a real feature of the world independent of how we think about it and perceive it. That does not mean that you think those things are not important. You may agree that *causality, wrong,* or *beauty* are concepts that are just as important to you as they are to those who interpret them the other way. *Of course* we use and need to use causal concepts and moral concepts, and so forth, you say. They are absolutely basic to thought and experience. There is no disagreement about that. The argument is over how to interpret their application to the world, and that is a philosophical task.

Taking the issue of beauty as an example may help. Everybody makes aesthetic judgments. We judge things to be beautiful or ugly, aesthetically worthy or trashy, and so forth. Do you think that beauty is in the eye of the beholder, that it is subjective, and that there are no objective criteria for what is beautiful? Or, is your view that standards of beauty are culture-bound? In that case, you maintain that different cultures have different notions of what is beautiful and that there is no neutral standpoint from which to judge whether any culture is right or wrong in its standards. On the other hand, you may hold that there are common, human standards of beauty but that they depend upon what human beings happen to be like. According to that view, beauty has no standing apart from how human beings perceive things, but we are talking about *human* perception, not the different individual, subjective perceptions of Bob, Carol, Ted, and Alice or the perceptions of this or that culture. There would be room to say that some individuals or some cultures are correct or mistaken in their judgments of beauty, but this would still be within boundaries set by human nature.

There is plenty of dispute between each of the views just identified, but every one of them is on one side of the divide we are beginning to map out. Whether beauty is person-relative, culture-relative, or human nature-relative, there is a dependence upon something about human beings (as individuals, members of groups, or members of a species). That is what makes all of these views distinct from views according to which beauty is a real, objective feature of objects independent of how people respond to them. If you are getting the sense of this major divide, then we are ready to introduce some important vocabulary.

If your position with respect to some issue (such as causality, wrongness, or beauty, for example) is that what is being talked about and thought about is independent of the *way* we talk and think about it, then your view is a **realist** view. If your view is that these things do not exist independently of our minds and our language, then you are an **antirealist. Realism** and **antirealism** are basic positions on the relations between what there is and thought and language.

Philosophers do not always use the terms "realism" and "antirealism" in discussing their views and developing their arguments. **Plato** (429–347 B.C.), Aristotle, Locke, **Hume** (1711–1776), and many other philosophers did not use precisely those terms, though they held positions to which the terms would apply. The terms are in fact used quite often in contemporary philosophy, but whether you encounter those two words or not is not the main point. What is crucial is the distinction between realism and antirealism to which the terms refer. It locates important groups of claims, arguments, and assumptions on the different sides of a fundamental divide. This distinction can be an important part of the compass you use to find your way around in philosophy.

What would the realist view be like? There are many different interpretations of realism. After all, this is philosophy. The interpretations share some important general features, however. For example, in the context of aesthetics, the realist maintains that beauty is a real feature of certain things. Some things have this feature and other things lack it, and its presence is not dependent upon how we judge things. We can be correct or mistaken in our judgments of beauty, and the bases for being correct or mistaken are real characteristics of the things judged. Just as, say, some things really are mammals or really are iron and not gold, some things really are beautiful and are not ugly or aesthetically indifferent. According to the realist regarding beauty, judgments of beauty are **realistically** true or false. They are not just matters of personal taste or culture-bound standards.

The realist discussing causality makes an analogous claim. The best interpretation of causality, argues the realist, is to understand it as a real relation between things. The use of causal concepts is a way of getting at what is really going on in the world; it is not merely a way that we interpret or conceptualize things. The same can be said of the concept *wrong* or the concept *right* in moral thought on the realist view. The best interpretation of them, says the realist, is one according to which they refer to real features of actions.

The antirealist might agree that the concept of causality is of the greatest importance, yet might also argue that causal thinking is a way that we organize our experience and not a way of reporting a real feature of things "out there." A moral antirealist might argue that *of course* moral judgments are of the greatest importance, but they do not report moral "facts." Moral judgments are to be interpreted, perhaps, in terms of human sensibility and responses.

The realist/antirealist debate is a distinctively philosophical one and one of the most important ones, too, because it is a debate about the relation between mind and world at a very general, abstract level. A dispute about whether a certain disease is caused by a bacterium or by a virus is a debate within science. The argument over whether execution should be the punishment for a certain crime is a debate within morality (and politics). The debate about whether a musical composition such as "Highway to Hell" by AC/DC ranks with Beethoven's Ninth Symphony as a work of musical art is a debate within aesthetics, but the realism/antirealism debate is one that ranges across all of these debates.

Of course, we should not just *decide* whether to be a realist or an antirealist without carefully examining the strengths and weaknesses of each of the positions. Some of the most important argumentative moves in philosophy are moves in this debate because so much hangs on the commitments we make concerning it. Whether you are a realist or an antirealist should emerge from your consideration of the strengths and weaknesses of different ways of interpreting the matters at issue. For example, we need to see what interpretation of wrongness fits best with the ways in which moral perplexity or moral disagreements are resolved. Does it seem that changes in moral beliefs over time are best explained in realist (or antirealist) terms? There are always quite specific avenues of inquiry that can be pursued in considering the merits and liabilities of realism and antirealism. The distinction is an abstract and general one, but the moves we make that put us on one side or the other should be very careful, precise moves.

One reason to make the moves very carefully is that it is not necessary to be a realist (or an antirealist) about everything. It is possible to be a realist about causality but not about right and wrong. Similarly, you might be a moral realist but not an aesthetic realist. It is crucial to examine the reasons in each context where the dispute can arise. You might conclude that you are a moral realist but not a comic realist. Then your view would be that moral properties are real, but you have reasons for holding that whether something is funny or not depends wholly upon our responses. When we find something funny, you argue, we are expressing our reaction, not making an objective discovery. Morality, however, is different from that. This is not just because morality is more important than humor. Remember, to be an antirealist about something is not a way of holding that it is unimportant. Something can be *really* or *very* important without being interpreted realistically.

As you become more comfortable using the notions of realism and antirealism you will see how helpful they are in recognizing and illuminating the character of your own commitments on several issues. This should not be surprising, since the issue of the relation of mind to world is such a basic one. Now that we have identified this key issue, let's go on and work our way towards some other issues that are connected with it. Our discussion so far has supplied an entry point into a number of other issues, and we will proceed by identifying them and using each in turn as an entry into the next. We will start with an issue that is very down to earth.

Properties and Natural Kinds

Everyone will agree that iron and gold are among the inventory of nature, and of course, the concept iron applies to things that are pieces of iron and the concept gold applies to things that are pieces of gold. What then, is the problem? Philosophically, there *is* a problem. We have concepts (*iron* and *gold*) each of which applies to many particular things. (One of them applies to all of the pieces of iron; the other applies to all of the pieces of gold.) So, on the one hand, there is *particularity* (this piece of iron, this piece, and that one) and on the other hand there is *generality* (the concept applies in general to anything which is iron or a piece of iron). How are we to understand the relation between the *general* and the *particular*?

Do all of those things we recognize as iron count as iron *because* we apply a specific concept to them, or is the correct application of the concept a matter of what those individual things *are*? It almost certainly will not do to simply say "It is iron if we *say* that it is iron." After all, why then would we say it of this one thing but not of that other thing? So, it is not just a verbal matter. You are free to say "This substance is not poison if I say that it is not," but that will not stop it from making you sick or even killing you if you ingest it. How are we to account for the fact that concepts have general applications? What we need to clarify is who is leading in the dance of mind and world. Is it the world or is it the mind, or, is there some option that involves both, without either one clearly leading on its own?

We perceive *particulars*. We perceive this particular red shirt, that red stop sign, or that red tomato sauce but we think *in general*. We use the concept *red* to refer to all of those particulars. One possibility is to argue that there are general features of reality; that generality is *real* (that is, it is to be interpreted realistically). There is something that makes all of the particular things that are iron, iron. There is some real property that is shared by them. One of them is not more or less iron (though it might be more or less pure iron) than another, and it is the same real property that is common to all things which are iron. Properties, says this view, are real and common and there are real *natural kinds* of things.

That might seem obvious. After all, why else would we apply the concept to some things and not to others? Yet, it is not obvious. There is another, quite different but also plausible, account of the application of the concept. The antirealist will argue that the application of the concept is not arbitrary, but it is not to be explained on realist grounds, either. We use concepts to pick out and refer to different kinds of things, but those kinds are not self-identifying. *We* do the classifying. The kinds of things that there are in the world do not show us what concepts to group them under. Yes, iron is different from gold, yet the distinctions we make between kinds of things depend upon how *we* employ concepts, and they are not fully determined by the world. The antirealist argues that there are kinds of things, but they are not real, natural kinds. To reinforce the plausibility of this, try the following.

Next time you are outside, look around and try to count how many things there are. One problem is that there are so many things, but the large number of things is not the philosophical problem. The really tricky issue is figuring out what *kinds* of things to count. You cannot just count *things*; you have to count things of this or that kind: plants, trees, oaks, leaves, animals, humans, birds, tables, green things, lawyers, round things, single parents, auto mechanics, and so on. You could easily spend the day constructing lists of kinds of things to count before you actually started counting any individual things. You might begin to wonder which of these kinds are real kinds and which are dependent upon our conceptual choices and ways of describing things. There are people who are aunts, and there are people who are uncles, so, why aren't there people who are *aunticles* (anyone who is either an aunt or an uncle)? We could use that concept to classify and count things. Why don't we?

That last category probably seems silly. Maybe trees are part of nature and tables are only artifacts, but there really are tables in a way that there are not really aunticles. Should we conclude that there is something wrong with antirealism because the aunticle example shows that there is a clear difference between real kinds and made-up kinds? Actually, the "aunticle" case does not threaten antirealism in quite that way. The antirealist is not obliged to assign aunticles and trees the same status even though he denies that we have access to objects independent of how we conceptualize them. You should consider what might be the antirealist's answer to the objection. In any event, what *is* the basis for dividing the world into different kinds of things?

Empirical inquiry can tell us whether there are any carnivorous birds, black holes in our galaxy, or any more gold in Alaska. Philosophical thinking is not the way to answer such questions, though the issue of whether there are real, natural kinds and shared properties is a *philosophical* matter. It may seem plain that there are no general things and that there are only particulars, but particulars are alike in their qualities and properties. Both a stop sign and a quantity of tomato sauce have the property *red.* So, is there some sense in which there *are* general things? To think or say anything about the world requires concepts. Can we, by the use of our concepts, say what there is independent of them? Are concepts (as the realist maintains) a means of access to the real order of things, to the properties and natural kinds that there are independent of concepts or, (as the antirealist maintains) is the order of things dependent upon the concepts that we use?

We mentioned above that it is perfectly all right to claim that some concepts are to be interpreted antirealistically and that some are to be interpreted realistically. For example, maybe you think that *iron* and *gold* are to be interpreted realistically, but that *stewing hen* and *fryer* (you will find these in the poultry section of your supermarket) are to be interpreted antirealistically. This is not a distinction grounded in the biological nature of the chickens. In that respect it is a *conventional* distinction rather than a real or natural one. Similarly, what is a foul ball and what is a fair ball in a baseball game depends upon the rules of baseball. "Foul ball" and "fair ball" are not natural kinds in the way that iron and gold are and neither are the kinds named by the terms "lawyer," "accountant," "nurse practitioner," "pastry chef," or "embalmer."

This might make it seem that there is a fairly direct route out of our quandary, namely, that there are artificial kinds and there are natural kinds. For example, "mayor" names an artificial kind, while "human being" names a natural kind. Perhaps we should say that the former are to be interpreted antirealistically and the latter are to be interpreted realistically. It is not that simple, and here is why. The fact that we are talking about something that occurs in nature and which is not an artifact does not on its own settle the matter of whether the boundary of that kind of thing is drawn by nature or by us. After all, surely you can imagine using a different set of concepts to classify the things in the natural world. Different cultures and different theories do just that. The fact that the elements of a set of concepts "work" does not show that they are realistically the right ones. Many different sets of concepts can "work." There can be rules for their proper use, and we can tell when people use them correctly and when they do not, yet that does not resolve the realism/antirealism debate. To do that, we need to keep doing philosophy.

There are many different versions of realism and antirealism. That is, in part, what sustains the life of philosophical reflection. Different ways of understanding the status of moral and aesthetic values, natural kinds, qualities such as colors, or relations such as causation are developed, criticized, and revised. There is an ongoing reflective, critical project of trying to understand the mind-world relation and also the language-world relation.

We mentioned above that to have an antirealist position on a specific issue is not at all the same thing as holding that it is simply a matter of subjective opinion or that there is no real difference between being correct and being mistaken about it. Suppose you are a moral antirealist. You may not think that there is a property of being morally right or being morally wrong that is somehow built into the world, independent of human concerns, interests, and feelings. You could still maintain that some things are right and others are wrong and that people can be mistaken or correct about such matters. The antirealist and the realist may even agree on moral issues. Both can maintain that it is wrong to make deceitful promises, that it is good to aid those in distress, that justice and courage are virtues. Nothing stands in the way of them agreeing on what specific sorts of actions justice and courage require. Their disagreement is over the *status* of moral claims. Do they refer to moral facts? Do they express judgments grounded in human sensibility? There may be a good deal of "content" agreement but disagreement over what underwrites that content.

The dispute between the realist and the antirealist is a dispute about whether the facts that support a claim are mind-independent facts or not. Can our concepts register what there is and what it is like in its own right, or do the distinctions between kinds depend upon how we conceptualize them? Are there shareable properties? Are there moral facts? Is causality an objective, real relation? Are there rights that people have just by virtue of being human beings, or are rights always created by human convention? Are the entities that scientific theories refer to (such as quarks, electrons, and genes) real entities, or are they theoretical fictions that are useful for organizing and explaining more observable phenomena? These are all ways of raising the question of realism and antirealism.

It is helpful to stop and ask oneself, "What does this philosopher interpret realistically, and what does this philosopher interpret antirealistically, and why?" It is a good question to ask yourself because it is an effective way to discover your own general views and how well they fit together.

The debates about realism and antirealism are connected with a number of other basic philosophical issues. We are going to look at some of those issues now and trace some of the connections.

The Nature of Necessity

One of the issues we mentioned in chapter 1 was whether there are properties that an object *must* have in order to be what it is. For example, is it necessary that a human being be a mammal? Is it necessary that copper have atomic number 29? Must a square have four sides? This question of what is necessary versus what is not necessary marks a basic distinction. If your position is that some properties are necessary, that there are properties which things of given kinds *must* have, then you are a realist about necessity. This position is often called **essentialism**. In this view, the difference between the properties that a thing must have and the ones it can exist without is a real difference, grounded in reality, and not in how we describe or conceptualize these properties.

On the other hand, if you hold that the question about what properties things must have is answered in terms of the concepts or language that we use, you are an *antirealist with respect to essences*. Your view might be that the classification of things into different kinds depends upon conceptual choices. That seems quite plausible. After all, we *could* classify things differently. Still, maybe it seems plain to you that if something is a human being it *has to* be a mammal. You have the conviction that it could not be human if it is not mammalian. That seems plausible too. Where philosophical reflection gets to work is in considering what kind of *has to,* or what kind of necessity, that is.

Consider the following statements. Do they seem to express claims that are necessary or not?

> Iron is a metal.
> Dogs are animals.
> There are penguins in the Antarctic.
> Automobiles are artifacts.
> Red is a color.
> If X is a stone, then X is a stone.
> Parrots (typically) live longer than hummingbirds.
> Murder is wrong.
> 11 is an odd number.
> Three strikes and you are out.
> If a match is soaking wet, it will not light.

None of these appears to be philosophically significant in terms of content, yet reflection on them raises important philosophical issues. There are several things to consider. First of all, are the statements true? Of those that are true, do some of them seem to you to express necessary truths? If so, do they seem to express the *same kind* of necessity?

There could be several kinds of necessity. Suppose there is a kind of necessity grounded in the nature of things. We might call that *real* or *metaphysical* necessity. An example of that might be that dogs are animals. This, it could be argued, is not just a matter of how we use words, it is a matter of what it is to be a dog. What about *linguistic* or *definitional* necessity? That would be necessity structured by linguistic conventions, by rules for the use of words. Perhaps "uncles are male" is an example of linguistic necessity. In order to know how to use the word "uncle" properly, you need to understand that uncles are males, but this isn't any sort of necessary fact about the nature of things. In what ways, if any, do the "dogs are animals" and "uncles are male" cases seem to be different? If you think that there are examples of real necessity *and* also examples of linguistic necessity, how do you discriminate between them? Is linguistic necessity revisable? "All swans are white," has been regarded as an example of linguistic necessity, but it turns out that it is not even true. That raises questions about whether it was *ever* necessary or whether it was just thought to be necessary. Was it necessary in the past but not now?

There is also *logical* necessity—the necessity of (All X are Z) following from [(All X are Y) and (All Y are Z)]. This is usually regarded as being strictly formal, a matter of the logical structure of statements and arguments. Remember, if an argument form is logically valid (and our example *is* logically valid), then the conclusion follows necessarily from the premises. This is a matter of structure rather than the content of the statements that supply the premises and conclusion. If a statement is logically necessary, then any statement of that form is logically necessary. For example, any statement of the form "If A then A" is logically necessary. Now consider the statement "Water, at normal atmospheric pressure, boils at 100 degrees Celsius." This statement is true, and we have knowledge of the relevant laws of nature that explain the process of water changing its state in that way. It is true, but it is not *logically* necessary. It may be *causally* necessary. Though boiling is a necessary effect of heating to that temperature, it is necessary *given the laws of nature.* Given the laws of nature, there are certain definite causal relations between specific kinds of events. Logical necessity is not tied to the actual laws of nature in the way that causal necessity is. If something is logically necessary it is necessary no matter what else is the case. What is logically necessary stays the same even in a world in which the laws of nature are different—where there are unicorns, elves, and smoking is good for you.

You might hold that it is necessary that dogs are animals, though it is not necessary that there are dogs. In fact, there *are* dogs, and nothing which is a dog could fail to be an animal (the argument goes), but that there are dogs at all is not a necessary truth. It is *contingent.* It is contingent that World War II ended in 1945. It is contingent that a man walked on the moon in 1969. It is contingent that dinosaurs are extinct. It is contingent that General Motors is a larger corporation than Hewlett Packard. It is contingent that you were born and that you have a specific name. If something is possible, but not logically necessary, it is contingent.

One topic of ongoing philosophical debate is the question of the relations between **metaphysical, logical**, and **causal** necessity. Are they three distinct kinds of necessity, or are they really all variants of one kind? One of the problem areas is this: It does not seem that everything which is causally necessary is also logically necessary (recall the boiling water example). What about the relation between causal and metaphysical necessity? Are they distinct? Are causal and metaphysical necessity *weaker* than logical necessity? What precisely would that mean? After all, if something is necessary, it is necessary. Do we need to qualify that claim to show which kind of necessity we mean? You might want to go back over the list above and pick out the entries you take to be necessary, and try to explicate what kinds of necessity you find.

It is worthwhile to consider why questions about necessity are fundamental in philosophy. Addressing the question of what *must* be the case, and also the question of what *cannot* be the case, is a way of gaining an understanding of the most basic structure of reality, or at least the most basic structure of how we think about it. We often make claims about what *must* happen or about what *cannot* happen. Think, for example, of some of the stories in the tabloids for sale at the supermarket. When you see a story about a five-year-old child giving birth to twins, you think, "That's impossible." What kind of impossibility is that? Clearly, the story defies the limits of causal possibility. Given what we know about how the world works, such an event cannot occur. Is it, however, logically possible?

Maybe necessity is just one thing, or maybe there really are different kinds of necessity. This is a topic rich with opportunities for philosophical inquiry and very wide-ranging in its importance.

Necessity and Knowledge: The Roles of Reason and Sense

The debate about necessity is not just a debate about the nature of reality. It is also a debate about the possibility and nature of *knowledge* because questions about the nature of reality are connected with questions about how we can (*if* we can) know reality. As your study of philosophy progresses, you will notice that there are some philosophers who claim that there is a necessary structure to reality and that we can have knowledge of it. Among them are Plato, **Descartes** (1596–1650), **Spinoza** (1632–1677), and **Hegel** (1770–1831). The views of these thinkers have certain abstract affinities even though their works are different in many important respects. Philosophers who claim that there is a necessary structure to reality and that we can have knowledge of it also argue that *reason* or *intellect* is a faculty that yields knowledge and that sense perception, at best, yields confused and incomplete knowledge. There are several important thinkers who have held that reason enables us to grasp and understand the real, essential nature of reality. We will work our way toward an explanation of this common feature of their views as follows.

Think about a claim such as, "A triangle is a three-sided figure," and compare it to a claim such as, "There is an elephant in the zoo in Syracuse, New York." How do we ascertain if these are true? We could ask people. It's not that we should take a poll or a survey, but you could ask someone who knows some geometry, and you could ask someone who knows about the zoo in Syracuse. A great deal of what we believe or even claim to *know,* we accept on the authority of others. What we are asking about here is how would you come to know such things in the first place, at the origin of that knowledge, so to speak?

The claim about triangles is known to be true on different kinds of grounds from the claim about the zoo. The latter is an empirical claim, known to be true or false on the basis of evidence accessible to the senses. We cannot ascertain whether it is true or not just by an exercise of reason. We need empirical support for it. That is an evidence gathering job that relies at some point on sense perception or observation.

On what basis do we have knowledge of the properties of triangles? That seems to be knowledge grounded on something other than sense perception. It can be helpful to look at pictures or models of triangles in order to better understand them, though that is an aid to knowledge which is not itself perceptual knowledge. What kind of knowledge is it? One important view is that it is a claim of reason. We do not just make it true by definition, and we do not discover it on the basis of sense perception. It is known to be true by the operation of reason or intellect. This has also been asserted for claims such as the following: "There is no largest prime number," "All events have causes," "The mind and the body are distinct substances," "Justice is a virtue," and "Red is a color." These claims exhibit considerable variety of subject matter, but they are all examples of the sorts of claims that have been offered as candidates for being claims of reason, known on grounds independent of evidence acquired by sense perception.

Moreover, they are examples of the sorts of claims that many philosophers have held to be necessary truths. According to this view, reason enables us to have knowledge of truths that are not based upon evidence obtained by sense perception and that are not just a matter of conventions of language. What about "No square is a rectilinear figure," or "Seven is evenly divisible by two," or "No physical object occupies any space"? Those are all false and necessarily false. If we can know what is necessarily true by reason alone, we can also recognize necessary falsehoods by reason alone. There is, in the view of many philosophers, an important connection between necessity and reason.

Why should this be? It has often been maintained that reason or the intellect can recognize and understand *general* truths and connections that are not accessible to sense perception. By the senses, we perceive *particulars;* we perceive this red scarf, that long mustache, that snow-covered peak, and so on. It is by the use of reason that we understand what is general or universal. It is by the use of reason that we understand the connection between being a three-sided enclosed figure and being a triangle, between being extended in space and being a material thing, and between being a mammal and being an animal. Whether there is a chair in the next room is found out on the basis of sense perception. There might be, and there might not be. Even if there is one, it is not a necessary truth that the chair is in that room. It could be argued, however, whether the claim that anything that occupies space is a physical object is a claim of reason. You only need to consider the concepts of occupying space and physical object to see that this is true. No empirical investigation is required. Not only that, but these general connections are held to be necessary. They are claims about what must be so and what cannot be so. They cannot be strengthened by observation or defeated by it. If someone claims to have seen a four-sided triangle, we do not need to examine the triangle, just in case it really *is* a triangle with four sides. What we need to question is that person's understanding of what a triangle is.

We may draw a triangle or show someone a red scarf, a stop sign, and a spoonful of tomato sauce, as a way of illustrating a necessary connection (e.g., that triangles are three-sided enclosed figures and that red is a color). The particular example that we perceive helps us to understand the general point. What is understood by examining a particular case is both general and necessary, even though that particular experience was the occasion for achieving the understanding. Sense perception can facilitate rational knowledge, but the knowledge is an achievement of reason. This view has a long and distinguished tradition. It is not the "official doctrine" of philosophy, but it is one important perspective on a fundamental debate about necessity and knowledge. That debate is right at the heart of the entire history of Western philosophy. It is related to another issue, also very old but very much alive in our time. This is the issue of *certainty.*

Knowledge and Certainty: Rationalism and Empiricism

Many philosophers maintain that there is an important connection between necessity, reason, and certainty. Two philosophers who believe this are Plato and Descartes, whose views illustrate an important point of contact between debates about knowledge and debates about reality. They argue that *only* reason can yield knowledge, and it can yield *certain* knowledge. Indeed, according to some philosophers, if a claim is less than certain it is not a genuine or successful knowledge-claim. We can have knowledge because we possess reason, and it is reason alone which is a faculty of genuine knowledge. Why should there be this connection between necessity, reason, and certainty?

Here we need to make some distinctions between different kinds of certainty. Sometimes we take something to be certain because it is too psychologically disturbing not to; we want to believe it and it "costs" too much not to. Maybe it is too painful to believe that something terrible has happened to a loved one, so you persist in denial. That kind of certainty will not yield knowledge. Maybe you hope that something (over which you have no control) will come true. You believe that it will, and you anticipate how great you will feel when it does. Then when it happens, you say, "I was certain it would happen; I knew it." Yet, the hope that it would happen is a different state of mind than having adequate evidence that it would. When you confidently announce (in May) that such and such a team will win the next World Series, and then they do in fact win, you might boast, "You see, I knew it all along." Of course you did *not* know it all along, even though your belief was true. How *could* you have known? Keep this in mind if you are considering subscribing to a stock market analyst's newsletter.

As a feature of a knowledge-claim, certainty is not just a matter of subjective conviction or the strength of hope, wishful thinking, or even true belief. It is possible to have a true belief about something and still lack knowledge of it. If your belief is unsupported by evidence, or you only have the belief because it makes you feel better, then you still lack knowledge. There are several types of psychological certainty which do not pass the tests that must be met in order for a belief to count as certain *knowledge* (if indeed any does).

You will probably agree that you know that "Mammals are animals," that "Seven is an odd number," that "There are some physical objects on the surface of the earth," and that "London is north of Rome." If you also claim to be certain of these things, what is the basis of that claim? If you are certain, does that mean that you cannot be mistaken, that nothing else you could find out could alter your belief (for good and relevant reasons), and that your grounds for belief are adequate? That sounds like a reasonable, preliminary characterization of certainty. Your belief is true, you believe it on adequate grounds, and no other belief you have or might acquire will give you reason to doubt it. Perhaps if those conditions are satisfied, you are certain in the sense that you cannot be mistaken. We will not pursue the issue of whether this is exactly right as a rendering of certainty. Instead, we will use that characterization as a working hypothesis for purposes of illustration.

Does anything you claim to know meet these conditions? They are, after all, quite strong conditions. Do you know (in that strong sense) what you had for breakfast this morning? Are you certain that you are reading a book about philosophy right now? Do you have *no conceivable doubt* that ounce for ounce, gold is more precious than iron? Are you sure that your parents have not moved without telling you? Are you absolutely certain that they would not do that? You may find that your confidence in many knowledge-claims and in whole classes of knowledge-claims is eroded by reflection on the questions we have raised.

One stance is that general, necessary truths knowable by reason alone can be known with certainty, while perceptual claims, memory claims, and other claims that need evidence from outside the intellect are vulnerable to too many grounds for doubt. We are subject to perceptual illusion, unreliable memory, and so forth. Real knowledge (genuine knowledge) has its source in the intellect. This, anyway, is the central claim of one tradition of thought, the *rationalist* tradition. Philosophers in the rationalist tradition (such as Plato and Descartes) argue that reason enables us to have knowledge of real necessities, and they also argue that only rational knowledge is *certain* knowledge. That is the connection between reason, necessity, and certainty that we discussed above.

John Locke, David Hume, and **A. J. Ayer** (1910–1989), to just name three, are leading figures in the *empiricist* tradition. Empiricists argue that sense perception is a source of knowledge. Some argue that reason *and* sense perception are each sources of different kinds of knowledge. Other more radical empiricists argue that *only* sense perception is a source of knowledge. It is by sense perception that we are informed about what there is in the world and what it is like. How could reason alone, how could just *thinking* without the content of sense perception, yield knowledge of the world? We know what causes what on the basis of sense perception. Our discoveries of the laws of nature are made on the basis of observation. Our knowledge of the past, whether yesterday or one thousand years ago, is based on sensory evidence. How could we possibly have knowledge of any of these things except on the basis of experience?

The empiricist tradition is a rich one that includes many different interpretations of the conditions for knowledge-claims. There are, for example, empiricists who argue that even though knowledge of the world is based upon experience, it can be certain knowledge. Others argue that conditions for knowledge which demand certainty cannot be met, but that we can have fallible, though genuine, knowledge because surely we can have knowledge of a matter without absolute, unassailable certainty, with every conceivable ground of doubt eliminated. If we could not, then we would not know anything at all. Perhaps none of our knowledge-claims are certain; we should acknowledge that fact without it undermining our beliefs and knowledge-claims. What is common to all of these is the insistence that if we are to have any knowledge of things in the world, it will be knowledge based upon sensory evidence.

Empiricists want to know why rationalists are so confident that the senses are less reliable than reason as a source of knowledge. Of course there are ways in which our senses can be deceived and mistaken, but often we can also find out whether we are mistaken or not. Surely reason can make mistakes, as well. Perhaps neither reason nor the senses is altogether reliable. Perhaps we should acknowledge that no knowledge-claims are absolutely certain, utterly free of any conceivable doubt.

We might want to reconsider our suggested conditions for knowledge and formulate other, less demanding ones. It may be that certainty is not a necessary condition of knowledge. That is an issue that needs careful consideration. It could also turn out that, in fact, we have very little knowledge or even none at all. That does not mean that we do not or should not have *beliefs*. Having no beliefs is hardly an option. We would carry on just as we do now but with the awareness that our beliefs are not up to the rigorous standards of genuine knowledge. Just because we have formulated what we take to be the right conditions for knowledge does not mean that anything satisfies those conditions. Sure enough, for as long as people have theorized about knowledge, there have been those who have held that we do not know anything or even that we *cannot* know anything. They are **skeptics**.

Skepticism

We noted above that one possibility is that neither reason nor sense-perception is completely reliable or trustworthy as a source of knowledge. Moreover, when we are talking about knowledge, we are not only talking about things such as mathematics and the perceptual knowledge of objects that we presently perceive. There are also the issues of memory, knowledge of the past, knowledge of the future, self-knowledge, and knowledge of unobserved facts. For example, when we say "all dogs are mammals," we are including dogs we have not observed and dogs that we will never observe. What about introspective knowledge and knowledge of our own states (physical and/or mental)? Examples of this include the possibilities of whether you have knowledge of your own desires, motives, beliefs, intentions, and so forth, and whether you are cold or are hungry, sitting cross-legged, or are awake or asleep.

In fact, one of the most important skeptical arguments is built on the basis of questions about dreaming. Descartes, in his *Meditations on First Philosophy,* asks himself if he knows what the marks are that distinguish dream-experiences from waking-experiences. Descartes himself was not a skeptic. In fact, he thought that we could achieve quite extensive knowledge that meets very demanding conditions of certainty. Still, he believed that it was essential to meet and defeat the strongest conceivable skeptical objections to knowledge-claims. Success at that would mean that knowledge-claims would be immune from doubt. One of his requirements for success was that he should be able to tell whether his experiences are dream-experiences or waking-experiences. This is a way of asking, "How can I know that my perceptions are perceptions of a real world external to my mind?" Without a satisfactory answer to this question, the shadow of doubt would be inescapable. Reflection on dreaming motivates questions about a skeptical challenge all of us can recognize. Descartes argued that we must meet it and defeat it, or we will not have the right to claim that we have knowledge.

Descartes' argument is an excellent example of how important justification is in philosophical inquiry. We all make a distinction between dreaming and being awake, and we all believe that we make the distinction quite successfully. Yet, it is very difficult to clarify just what the marks *are* by which we distinguish them. A dream experience can be as vivid and as convincing as a waking experience. How are you able to tell whether you are awake or dreaming, and are you able to specify how you can tell? Your beliefs may be true, but if they are not adequately justified, they may not count as *knowledge.*

Descartes' problem was philosophical not psychological. His primary concern was not that he might actually be dreaming, but that he might not be able to justify the claim that he was not. It is one thing to have true beliefs and another to have knowledge. Moreover, instead of dealing with skeptical challenges piecemeal, he wanted to take on the most radical, most global skeptical challenge and solve the problem of justification with a single systematic strategy. Tackling the concern about dreaming was part of doing so. Questions about individual knowledge-claims could still arise. After all, we could still be occasionally subject to deception, unreliable memory, and so forth. Yet, if the overall skeptical challenge in its most menacing form is defeated, then we can be confident that it is possible to correct errors without calling into question the very possibility of knowledge.

One issue raised by Descartes' approach to the problem of knowledge is whether his very strong conditions for knowledge are ever met. Another issue is the question of whether that very strong standard is the right one. Do those conditions *need* to be met? That is what a good deal of **epistemology** is about. Epistemology is the philosophical examination of the possibility, scope, and nature of knowledge.

We saw earlier that you can be a realist about some matters and an antirealist about others. Similarly, you can be a skeptic about some kinds of knowledge-claims and nonskeptical in other areas. It is also possible to be a global or radical skeptic and to hold that we have no knowledge of *anything*. Some skeptics argue that not only do we *in fact* not know anything, but we *cannot* have knowledge of anything. They argue that given our cognitive abilities and the conditions of knowledge, it is not possible for any claims to fully meet those conditions. Some of the most important work in the history of philosophy is work aimed at articulating, meeting, and defeating skeptical challenges. The very issue of what sort of skeptical challenge(s) should worry us is a fundamental philosophical question.

This was an issue in antiquity, and it is an issue today, which is unsurprising. If philosophy is in large part the project of being self-consciously intellectually responsible, a very important part of philosophy will be the attempt to show whether, how, and to what extent knowledge is possible. We cannot, in good intellectual conscience, simply assert, "Of course there is knowledge and everybody knows that there is." Formulating and meeting skeptical challenges is a way of regulating our claims so that our confidence and convictions are not misplaced.

Most of the time this is not a pressing concern. In most contexts we accept claims made by others, and our own claims are accepted unless there is a special reason to question them. The skeptical concern does not ordinarily intrude into our thoughts and conversation. Still, there are skeptical questions that can be raised in many different contexts with which we are already familiar prior to philosophical reflection.

1. Is it possible to have knowledge of reality as it is in itself and not just as it appears to us in experience? (This is the question of **appearance and reality**.)
2. Is it possible to have knowledge that other people's minds and experiences are at all like our own? We observe people's behavior, but how can we know whether what goes on "in their heads" is comparable to what goes on in our own? (This is the **other minds** problem.)
3. Can inferences from observed cases to unobserved cases be rationally justified?(This is the problem of **induction**.)
4. Do people act only and always on the basis of self-interested considerations, or do they sometimes act out of impartial concern for others? (This is the problem of **moral motivation**.)
5. Are there objective moral considerations and can we have knowledge of them? (This is the question of **moral cognitivism**.)

With respect to each of these and more, there are important skeptical challenges. Granted, we generally do not raise these issues in systematic, sustained ways, yet we can see that the issue of skepticism is as wide in its scope as the realism/antirealism debate. It is related to that debate in that skeptical concerns focus on claims about the relation of mind and language to world. For any type of realist claim, there can be skeptical challenges aimed at showing that the claim exceeds what is available to justify it.

This should not give you the impression that the skeptic always has the last word. One type of response to a skeptical challenge is to argue that it is incoherent or in some way contrived. **Thomas Reid** (1710–1796) addressed skeptical challenges in this way. So did **Ludwig Wittgenstein** (1889–1951). Both of them developed deep insights about the possibility and nature of knowledge and the relation of mind and language to the world. They did not simply ignore or dismiss skeptical challenges. Instead, they sought to explain why they are based on a misunderstanding or how they might be self-defeating. They wanted to show that the concepts and language that we use are intelligible only if we live, think, and use words in a public world of objects and other people. If that is true, then certain kinds of skeptical challenges could not be successfully mounted in the first place. This is because our thoughts and beliefs presuppose a common world, shared with other thinkers as well as the objects that we think and speak about, and an ability to meaningfully communicate with other people.

Communication is important because, for a great deal that we claim to know, we rely upon the say-so, or authority, of others. By "authority" I do not mean that the other person must be an expert with some sort of specialized knowledge; I mean that instead of finding out a matter for ourselves, we find out from a person or from a source that we take to be reliable. Each of us "knows" that O. J. Simpson was acquitted in his criminal trial, and if we were not present in the courtroom when the verdict was read, we know it on the authority of others, as with our claim to know that the earth is approximately 93 million miles from the sun and that Napoleon was defeated at Waterloo on June 18, 1815. These are not things that we have come to know on our own except in the sense that we might have looked them up or asked someone who would know. There is a great deal that we accept on authority, take for granted, or that we figure that everybody "knows."

It is a very sobering exercise to stop and ask yourself, "What grounds do I have for claiming to know that?" Part of this exercise should be to make the needed distinctions between different kinds of knowledge-claims and the different kinds of grounds for them. This will illuminate the way in which the skeptical challenge is not just one thing. It may arise in different ways in different contexts, and it may need to be met in different ways. Perhaps, as Reid and Wittgenstein argued, it is itself based upon a misunderstanding or a misrepresentation of what is needed to justify knowledge-claims.

Our discussion so far has identified some of the most general philosophical issues. The realist-antirealist debate, the debates about the nature of necessity, the role of reason in knowledge, and the debate about certainty and skepticism are keys to the philosophical mapping of several problem areas. These abstract debates shape the more "local" philosophical issues at different places on the map. We turn now to another philosophical issue of very wide generality. It too arises in several areas of inquiry and reflection. This is the issue of *value*. Questions about the nature of value and about what things have value and in what ways, are **normative** questions. They arise almost everywhere.

Facts and Values

We cannot hope to cover or even introduce all of the issues about value that invite philosophical reflection and inquiry. We can, however, indicate and illustrate some of the most important kinds of questions. We will begin with something that is probably familiar and which may seem to be unproblematic. This is the distinction between fact and value.

When we say, "A given volume of iron is heavier than an equal volume of air," that is undoubtedly a factual statement. "Slavery and indentured servitude are unjust," is undoubtedly a normative claim, a claim about value. Can we, without problems, sort every claim into either the "fact" bin or the "value" bin? It is often thought so. Many people maintain that there is a clean break between describing (stating facts) and evaluating (expressing approval or disapproval, preferences, repugnance, and the like). For example, it is a fact that in the state of Texas more people have received death sentences than in Utah. Suppose you think that capital punishment is wrong or is an awful or barbarous practice. It could be argued that those thoughts (unlike the purely factual, descriptive claims about how many people are executed) express evaluations. Similarly, someone might agree that a certain food is nutritious on account of its vitamin and fiber content but also think that it is a disgusting thing to eat on account of its taste. That too seems to be a clear example of the distinction between facts and values. Maybe so, but there may be more complicated cases, or quite different kinds of relations between facts and values.

Here is an example. Suppose someone says, "It is the right kind of apple for the pie I want to make, but it is bruised." That is a factual claim, but it also makes an evaluative point. After all, you want a good pie, and you need good apples to make a good apple pie. The apples need to be *good* apples of the *right* kind. Indeed, someone might make the remark primarily with the intention of it being evaluative. The point of the remark is, "That apple does not meet the standards for ending up in one of my pies." It is open to you to argue that the apple being bruised is a factual matter, its not being acceptable for the pie is an evaluative matter, and that the two matters are distinct. Similarly, you could argue that it is a matter of fact what slavery is and how it affects people and so on and that the judgment that it is unjust is a distinct evaluative matter. Still, that position needs to be *argued for.* Even if it is true, it is not *obviously* true.

A somewhat different perspective on evaluative notions might run along the following lines. What makes a pie-apple a good one is different from what makes a Formula 1 race car a good one of its type, or what makes a refrigerator, a librarian, or a pilot a good one of its type. According to this view, the criteria for what makes something good depend upon what sort of thing it is. The criteria depend upon what is looked for, aimed at, or wanted in a thing of that kind. In that respect, there are factual considerations to take into account in making evaluative judgments. They are not arbitrary or unreasoned, and we can give supporting evidence for our judgments. Moreover, some people are expert judges of different things because of their knowledge of the relevant qualities. The expert at judging show-dogs has a quite different kind of factual expertise from the expert at judging automatic transmissions or missile-tracking radars. In each context there are real differences between competent and incompetent judging and between correct and incorrect evaluations.

At this point you might think, "Well, doesn't this show that indeed, values and evaluative judgments *are* objective? After all, there are factual criteria for our evaluations." The matter is not settled so quickly. We said that the view is that there are different criteria for the good of different things and that the criteria are shaped by what is looked for or wanted in things of a particular kind. We could argue that values are still fundamentally subjective because value judgments are grounded in our desires and interests. On the basis of those desires and interests we can formulate shared, public standards or criteria, but what makes those the appropriate criteria is a matter of our desires or interests, not anything about the objects themselves. Take away the human desires and interests, and the values vanish with them. If we try to answer the question, "Where in the world is value?" we find that ultimately it is grounded in our attitudes, desires, and responses; it is based in human subjectivity.

What we have just described is a version of a widely held position. Its core consists of three claims. First, there are facts, and factual claims are objective. Second, values are fundamentally subjective. Third, values are the result of *evaluations* and thus are determined by our approval, disapproval, likes, dislikes, and interests. Our value judgments *express* attitudes and responses. The apple is not good enough because of what we look for and approve of in pies. Slavery and indentured servitude are unjust because of what we look for in social systems. Maybe human interests, desires, and evaluations are widely shared, and this might help explain why there can be as much agreement as there is in evaluative judgments. The bottom line of this view, however, is that values are subjective.

This position is an example of how one can be an antirealist (or even a skeptic) about values, but this does not mean that "anything goes." There is still a difference between being correct and being mistaken in evaluative judgments, even if objective values are not built into, or "out there" in, the world. There are still norms that are the basis for whether our judgments are correct or not. So, even if values are in some basic sense subjective, there can still be shared, public standards of judgment. (Think of standards of taste in music, literature, and art.)

The relation between fact and value, or between describing and evaluating, is not always simple or obvious. Imagine that someone who has done something wrong blames another person who is known by her accuser to be innocent. Eventually we find this out. We might say something like, "That was a mean-spirited and dishonest thing to do. You *knew* she had done nothing wrong. You knew that you were the one to blame, yet still you blamed her, and she was punished. You ought to be ashamed of yourself." When we say of someone's act that it was "mean-spirited" and "dishonest" are we describing the act or evaluating it? It might seem that we are not merely describing it. After all, the way we talk indicates that we think it was a wrong thing to do and that it merits condemnation. At the same time, it might seem that we are not merely evaluating it without reporting facts about it. To say that it was "mean-spirited" and "dishonest" is to give information about it, which seems no less factual than saying "Her reputation was ruined by the accusation." Language is full of terms that seem to straddle facts and values. Consider, for example, "courageous," "undignified," "conscientious," "obnoxious," "healthy," "honest," and a whole host of others. If there *is* a sharp distinction between fact and value, philosophical reflection and analysis are needed to identify it. It is not always on the surface.

Consider the sentence about slavery and indentured servitude at the beginning of this section. When we say that those things are unjust, or are morally wrong because they are unjust, are we merely expressing our disapproval? That is a possibility worth exploring. On the other hand, you may believe that this is quite unlike the apples-for-the-pie case, and this is not only because it concerns something more important. It might seem to you that there are objective reasons for finding slavery and indentured servitude to be unjust and morally wrong. Indeed, one possibility is that the sentence states a *moral fact,* the fact that those things are unjust and morally wrong. Now, whether or not that is the right interpretation is a difficult question, and it is the sort of question that is addressed in moral philosophy and in **metaethics**. (Metaethics is theorizing about the semantics, epistemology, and metaphysics of moral value.) Our point is that it is not obvious that just because it is a sentence about values, it does not assert a fact. Again, we see that if there is a distinction between facts and values, it may be less of a clean break and less straightforward than you might think.

In addition, there are several different *kinds* of evaluation. Among them are moral evaluation, aesthetic evaluation, matters of personal taste (your favorite food or color, for example), and evaluation in terms of efficiency, convenience, or function. Accordingly, there are several different relevant *standards* of evaluation, and different considerations guide the types of normative judgment. Flogging may be an effective deterring punishment, but at the same time, it is morally unacceptable.

It rates high on one scale of value but not on another. A certain kind of car may be comfortable but excessively costly to operate. A certain drug may speed the healing process but also produce unpleasant side effects.

We can also see that it is not just that we think about issues that are normative issues, but thinking *itself* has a normative dimension. For example, when we are giving arguments, we are giving reasons in support of a claim; we are trying to give good reasons to accept the claim. Thus, even logic, which might seem purely technical, and little influenced by questions of value, has a normative dimension. After all, in logic we study what it is that makes an argument valid and what makes it strong or weak. A valid rule of inference is a *good* one because if we apply it correctly, we will not commit fallacies. A valid argument form will always lead us from true premises to a true conclusion, (though it cannot guarantee that the premises are, in fact, true). If you study logic, you will learn how to identify the formal structure of arguments and how to ascertain whether they are valid or not. In doing so, you are also evaluating the argument. If it is invalid, it is defective, fallacious, and in need of repair or replacement. Even though validity and invalidity are matters of precise rules and relations, they are also normative matters. Indeed, even the notion of *rationality* is a normative notion. It concerns what is involved in thinking and reasoning *well.* To be irrational or unreasonable is a defect of a certain kind. When we strongly disagree with someone, or when it is clear to us that there is an error in someone's reasoning, we may say such things as "You're crazy," or "That's just irrational." Those are negative evaluations. A sound knowledge-claim is one that is justified, and justification is a normative notion. Granted, in making these observations we are operating at a very high level of abstraction. Still, the altitude gives us a perspective from which to see that the issue of value, or what we can call *normativity,* is much broader in scope and is found in many more places than we initially suspected. Questions of value are by no means confined to morality, though that is where some of the most obvious and urgent ones are found.

Where We Are Now

We have noted how certain fundamental philosophical issues range across numerous contexts. There are also important connections between those issues. We can illustrate all of the main points of the chapter by reflecting on moral value. Questions about realism and antirealism certainly apply. We want to know if values are objective and if they are independent of our feelings, desires and attitudes. Questions about knowledge and certainty apply in the moral context. Is there moral knowledge, and if there is, what justifies a moral knowledge-claim? Are there moral truths that we can know with certainty? Are there necessary moral truths? What sorts of reasons are there for moral skepticism? In addition, questions about the relations between facts and values certainly apply. Are there moral facts? What is the relation of the value of an action or situation to facts about that action or situation? Questions like those point to important features of the abstract landscape of philosophy. On the one hand, you should be able to see that there are fundamental abstract issues that range across the contexts of different philosophical problems. On the other hand, you should also be able to see how, in any given area of philosophy, there are fundamental abstract issues of several kinds. Whatever the context in which a question has arisen there are certain philosophical concerns that are unavoidably part of the project of addressing it.

It makes a difference that you are able to see that this is so. Bringing these abstract features of issues into view better enables you to trace out implications of the various positions on them. The value and usefulness of that ability is not confined to the study of philosophy. It brings a level of clarity and rigor to whatever it is you think about, even if it has nothing directly to do with philosophical issues. As a result of developing a philosophical perspective, you will be able to evaluate and appreciate issues and problems more swiftly and precisely. Not only are philosophical issues everyone's business, but also, whatever your business is, the skills that philosophy demands of you will help you to do it better. Perspective that is abstract *and* clear is very effective at putting details into place in the larger picture of which they are parts.

We now have a sense of some ways in which philosophical issues are motivated and formulated. Your acquaintance with issues such as realism and antirealism, essentialism, skepticism, and the other key notions of the chapter should aid you considerably in understanding many of the most important argumentative moves that philosophers make and where they are headed when they make them. You should now have a sense of some of the most prominent features of the philosophical terrain. The next step is to look at some different methods of philosophical argument by which to negotiate the terrain. That is the task of chapter 3.

Some Things to Think About and Discuss

1. Suppose a skeptic argues that it is not possible to conclusively distinguish between dreaming and the waking state because we may just be dreaming that we have made the distinction. How can that kind of argument be met? Does it have to be met in order for us to know that we are not dreaming?
2. People in different societies (and sometimes within the same society) often have quite different values. Is that evidence for the thesis that values are not objective? How might a defender of the objectivity of values interpret the lack of universal agreement? Does it matter whether we are talking about moral values rather than aesthetic values, or are the cases comparable?
3. If a duck's egg hatches, a duckling will emerge from it. Bear cubs, sunflowers, and other things do not hatch from duck eggs. Is it impossible for a bear cub to hatch from a duck's egg, or does it just never happen? On what basis do we know that this never happens? Is it a matter of fact, a matter of definition, or a matter of the structure of reality? Can you explain the difference (if there is one) between what *never* happens and what *cannot* happen?

Key Philosophers and Texts

Aristotle (384–322 B.C.) *Nicomachean Ethics:* This is historically the most important presentation of a virtue-centered ethical theory. There is also a great deal of contemporary interest in virtue ethics and in Aristotle's work in particular.

A. J. Ayer (1910–1989) *Language, Truth and Logic:* This presentation of what is known as Logical Positivism is a classic of twentieth century empiricism.

René Descartes (1596–1650) *Meditations on First Philosophy:* This is a key work in the development of early modern philosophy, and its influence motivated many philosophers to focus attention on epistemological questions. Descartes' attempt to formulate, meet, and defeat the challenge of skepticism is one of the most important developments in theorizing about knowledge. This book is also important as a defense of rationalism and also innate ideas.

G. W. F. Hegel (1770–1831) *Phenomenology of Spirit:* This is one of the most important works of the nineteenth century, and it continues to be a landmark in the history of rationalism.

David Hume (1711–1776) *An Enquiry Concerning Human Understanding:* Hume's *Enquiry* is the culmination of the early modern British empiricist tradition and notable as a critique of rationalism. Hume's treatment of the issues of causality and also free will and determinism remain among the very most important work on those issues.

John Locke (1632–1704) *An Essay Concerning Human Understanding:* Locke's critique of Descartes' formulation of the skeptical challenge and defense of rationalism and innate ideas was crucial to the development of modern empiricism and realism.

Plato (429–347 B.C.) *Republic, Sophist, Parmenides, Theaetetus:* Plato's formulations of metaphysical issues, ethical issues, and questions about knowledge remain classics, both in respect of how he saw the problems and in his interpretations of what constitute solutions to them. His views involve realist and rationalist elements.

Thomas Reid (1710–1796) *Essays on the Intellectual Powers, An Inquiry:* Reid is one of the most important figures in British philosophy after Hume. He interpreted Hume (and others such as Locke) as having views that were both skeptical in their implications and untenable. He challenged what he thought were the skeptical premises of his predecessors.

Baruch Spinoza (1632–1677) *Ethics:* This work is a rationalist classic, bringing together metaphysics and ethics in an attempt to formulate one overall systematic account of reality.

Ludwig Wittgenstein (1889–1951) *Philosophical Investigations, On Certainty:* Wittgenstein's reformulations of problems of knowledge and the genuineness of skeptical challenges have had a major influence on twentieth century philosophy. In particular, his focus on language and an examination of the relation between thought and language have led to dramatic reassessments of traditional epistemological questions.

Chapter 3

They're Arguing Again

HOW DO PHILOSOPHERS FIND THEIR STARTING POINTS? HOW do they make some of their key moves? What sorts of evidence are appealed to in developing a philosophical position? We will take up these questions by looking at examples from several different areas of philosophical theorizing, including the problem of knowledge, ethics, and the explanation of human action.

Equipped with a sense of what philosophical arguments are about, we are ready to look at some conceptions of the *starting points* and *methods* of philosophical argument. Where you start matters a great deal, and there is a wide range of approaches to the issues with correspondingly different conceptions of what counts as relevant evidence. Often the main interest of a position is the route by which reasoning and arguments arrive at it.

Why Are We Arguing?

Arguments are crucial in philosophy, and a philosophical argument is different from other types of arguments. Sometimes when people are arguing they say such things as, "Look, I came here to discuss this with you, not to have an argument." Having an argument in that way is one way of not getting along. We have probably all heard, "That's that, and don't give me an argument." In this situation, arguing is regarded as disobedience or defiance of authority. The kinds of arguments we are familiar with in our everyday lives are sometimes heated disagreements or quarrels. In philosophy, arguments are crucial because supplying arguments and carefully considering and criticizing them are among the most important ways of being intellectually responsible and of seeking truth. Philosophical arguments are not quarrels; they are articulations of reasoning.

The strength of reasons and how they are organized are what count most in philosophical arguments. An argument can be effective in the sense that it *persuades* people even if it is not a strong argument in terms of giving good reasons for its conclusion. Watch out for arguments like that. We can be misled if a fallacy is hard to detect or if an argument influences us by playing on our hopes or fears, for example. In philosophy, we are looking for arguments that are effective because they are strong and not just persuasive.

It is even possible for an argument's conclusion to follow from its premises yet still not be a strong argument. It can be valid without really showing anything. This can happen when the premises are doubtful or at least one of them is false, or perhaps there are not adequate grounds for accepting the premises. Also, it sometimes happens that an argument is suspect because the premises lead to a conclusion that we have independent reasons not to accept. Maybe the reasoning is all right, but we know that the conclusion of the argument is false. In that case, we had better check the premises very carefully in order to find the problem. In another case, the argument might be trivial, not because it is about something unimportant but because it does not do the work it is intended to do. This may be because the argument is circular and assumes in its premises that which it claims to prove. Suppose you are told, "Anything that can be correctly described as a lie is wrong, because it is part of the meaning of the word 'lie' that lies are wrong." You then ask how we know that lying is wrong by definition, and you are told, "It is clear that lying is wrong by definition because lying is morally impermissible, and if something is morally impermissible, that just means that it's wrong." That should not satisfy you. You want to know why lying is impermissible (and, therefore, wrong), but that is just what is assumed by a premise of the argument. The argument does not lead you to that conclusion. It just moves in a circle.

There is also what we might call a "so what" argument—the premises give some reason for the conclusion, but the connection between them is not of the right sort or maybe it leaves the main issue still unresolved. Here is an example of an argument of that type. The conclusion is that seven is a prime number, and the premises are that a mathematics book which is known to contain no mistakes contains the claim that seven is a prime number, and it is a mathematics book that many mathematicians use when they teach. This might be a way of showing that you have a reliable source for your belief that seven is a prime number. It is not a very good argument for *proving* that seven is a prime number because it fails to give mathematical reasons for accepting the claim. It does not tell us how it is known that seven is a prime number in such a way that we can tell whether the book is accurate. This argument is not *entirely* irrelevant to the job it is used for, but it's not quite what we are looking for as reasoning about mathematics.

Arguments are so important in philosophy because in doing philosophy we cannot merely assert things, we need to *show why* they should be accepted, and the strength and relevance of the answer to the "why" question depends upon the reasons in favor of the claim. The development of a philosophical argument may proceed over dozens of pages or several chapters in which the reasoning aimed at a certain conclusion is presented. Generally, authors will *not* say, "All right, here is the argument," and just lay it out before us. Even in cases where the author does just that, the argument that is formally presented is the result of a good deal of reasoning that led to its economical, explicit formulation.

It is a great help to be able to identify or extract the *main* argument of a philosophical book, chapter, or article. This should be one of your primary concerns in reading philosophy. There are many arguments in say, Descartes' *Meditations on First Philosophy,* but there is also an important respect in which all six of its chapters develop one overall argument. Similarly with **Kant's** (1732–1804) *Critique of Pure Reason,* John Stuart Mill's (1806–1873) *Utilitarianism,* or Hume's *An Enquiry Concerning Human Understanding.* (Just as an observation here: Charles Darwin, in *The Origin of Species,* tells the reader that the book is "one long argument.") You have made an important step toward understanding the abstract architecture of philosophy when you can identify the main overall argument of a work and the way in which it makes a contribution to the larger debate of which it is part. When you are trying to identify the main, overall argument, you are trying to identify that author's distinctive contribution to the philosophical debate in which he or she is engaged.

Motive and Opportunity

When you read the work of a philosopher and your reaction is "This is crazy," or "This just cannot be right," you should always stop to consider *why* someone whose views seem to you to be crazy or obviously wrong is considered someone whose arguments are worth studying.

There is almost certainly something (and maybe there are several things) about the philosopher's argument that merits serious and sustained attention. Trying to understand the author's philosophical motivations will help you in your effort to understand philosophical writings. This is not a matter of imaginatively putting the author through psychoanalysis. It is a matter of seeing the texture and genuineness of the matter at issue so that you can begin to see the reasons why a thinker would start *there* and proceed in *that* manner.

A philosophical starting point is the difficulty or the perplexity that is felt regarding an argument and how this perplexity is formulated. Once it dawns on you why an author would assert *those sorts of things,* you are getting a sense of what is philosophically at stake. It is important to try to understand the perplexity, the philosophical concern that is motivating the author's arguments and claims. If you read a work of philosophy as a collection of statements untethered to that concern, you will find it much more difficult to appreciate. Once the problem or the perplexity that the author is wrestling with is recognized, you too can see the need to wrestle with it.

You must start somewhere, but there is not just one place where everyone must start. Perhaps you just are not very interested in the issue of personal identity, but the question of freedom of the will is interesting and important to you. Maybe the arguments about the possibility and nature of knowledge all seem remote and leave you cold, but you are intrigued by questions about moral value. Our interests ebb and flow at different places, but we should recall what we have said in the previous chapters:

1. Many philosophical issues are connected, and there are certain issues that come up in many different contexts. These are highly general issues about realism and antirealism, necessity, and normativity, among others. So, even if your interest is aroused only in a certain context, the skill you develop in thinking about those issues can be deployed in thinking about others.
2. Our views about one philosophical issue can have important consequences for our views about others. The whole philosophical fabric is involved even if we are just tugging on one thread.

Context and Content

Before we discuss different philosophical methods, we should say a little bit about the significance of the context in which a philosopher lives.

In an important way philosophy takes less for granted than other disciplines. After all, so much of philosophy is about fundamentals. Many things are called into question by philosophy which are not called into question by other disciplines. Even in philosophy, however, it would be impossible to start utterly without assumptions or presuppositions. Maybe those starting points will be revised or rejected further along in the inquiry, but we cannot expect even a philosopher to start without some assumptions. As you might expect, these are often shaped by the historical and cultural context in which a philosopher lives.

Recognizing this we might think, "Of course **Thomas Aquinas** (1225–1274) developed arguments for the existence of God; he was a medieval Christian theologian. Unless you share his starting points, there is not much to be gained by considering his arguments. Most of us do not now share his world-view, so his arguments can be dismissed." You might also think, "Maybe Kant claimed to identify the fundamental principle of morality, but he was being dogmatic and thought that the morality of his culture and time was objective morality." Along the same lines, you could think, "Aristotle was describing a flourishing human life in terms that reflected his place in ancient Athenian society. His notion of human virtue is relative to his social condition and is not true of human nature generally." This sort of list could continue and grow to be very long.

Knowledge of context can be helpful in understanding a philosopher's work, but it is not a substitute for a philosophical understanding of it. For example, John Locke lived during a period of upheaval and civil war in seventeenth-century Britain. It was a time during which an emerging commercial class was beginning to assert its political power, and the power of the monarchy and the landed aristocracy was being challenged. So, we might think that those circumstances strongly influenced Locke's theorizing about private property, limited government, and the right of revolution in order to protect natural rights. Why not interpret Locke as a spokesman for a particular class in the social and political struggles of his time and place? He certainly seems to have fulfilled that role. Yet, to look at his work *primarily* in that way risks becoming a way of *not* looking at his work philosophically. It would be remarkable for someone to have held Locke's views in twelfth-century Japan, for example. Still, insofar as there is philosophical substance and significance in Locke's work, it is on account of the merits of his arguments and analyses of issues. They were developed in a particular historical context, and they give us insights into how people of the day understood their world, but they are not merely symptoms of that context. Locke continues to be a participant in fundamental debates on the basis of the depth and strength of his reasoning. It would be a mistake to ignore or discount historical and sociological explanations of a thinker's motives and convictions. Nonetheless, we should guard against confusing these explanations with philosophical understanding.

Descartes provides another good example of this point. He developed his views about the nature of knowledge during a time of dramatic developments in theorizing about nature and scientific explanation. Also, there were intense controversies (and sometimes open warfare) about religious and political authority. There was a good deal of questioning at the most basic level, with respect to knowledge, faith, the principles of the political order, and other matters. It should be expected that in times like those *of course* someone would seek to identify and articulate the foundations of knowledge and try to put the new sciences on a firm footing. Well, yes, that does make sense, though the assessment of Descartes' project as a philosophical project is a separate matter. The power of his insights is a matter of how effectively they still figure, in our very different times, in the debate about the nature of knowledge. Indeed, they still figure very prominently.

There is one context that is always very important, and this is the one set by a philosopher's predecessors. This is not because philosophers lack originality. It is because of the persistence and genuineness of philosophical issues. The very formulation of a problem is influenced by the ways in which others have addressed it. Sometimes philosophers remark explicitly that a predecessor's work has been crucial to the development of their own thought. There is Kant's famous remark that reading Hume awoke him from his "dogmatic slumber." Aristotle refers explicitly, and respectfully, to his predecessors, **Socrates** (c. 470–399 B.C.) and Plato among them. Knowledge of the history of philosophy enables us to clearly see the affinities between different issues, the recurrent themes, and the points of contact between philosophers who, on the surface and by many measures, go about their work in quite different ways. The history of philosophy is the primary context of philosophy, and that is part of why even ancient philosophical works can still be of the first importance.

Varieties of Style and Method

Sometimes authors with very different styles are actually working on the same (or closely related) issues. The style is more than a literary feature. It can be an important aspect of argumentative strategy. For example, Plato wrote most of his works in the form of dialogues. This form gives a kind of life to the issues, as you see them develop in the course of conversations and as the participants in the conversations revise, reconsider, and reformulate their claims and respond to objections to them. Plato is a master at guiding us to very high levels of abstraction from conversational starting points that are down to earth. Instead of proceeding by saying, "Here is the issue, and here is my view of it," he proceeds by showing us how the issue emerges from concerns, questions, or views that many of us already have. His works are wonderful illustrations of something we remarked on in chapter 1, namely, that philosophical issues are issues for everybody and they are everywhere, including close to home.

A philosopher's mode of presentation can illuminate how he or she proceeds intellectually. It can be evidence of what that author thinks is the right way for an issue to arise, the right approach to it, and what counts as resolving it. Again, Plato is an excellent example of this. Often when people are engaged in dialogue, the thinking of each is changed along the way. They are not just reporting already formulated arguments to each other. They are working something out, and the dialogue itself is a process of illumination, discovery of error, and enlargement or refinement of perspective. The dialogue form itself tells us something about Plato's view of how our minds can be changed in the direction of deepening knowledge.

We can further illustrate the significance of style and method by contrasting some of the works of Aristotle and Descartes. When you read works by Aristotle, you may notice that he often begins by indicating the prevailing view of an issue, what is accepted as the opinion of the wise, or what is the way that things *seem.* A clear example of this is Book I of the *Nicomachean Ethics.* (Nicomachus was either someone who edited the work or a person to whom it was dedicated. Often this work is referred to in the way we will refer to it here, simply as the *Ethics).* The *Ethics* is an investigation of what is the best kind of life for a human being and what sorts of characteristics a person needs to live that sort of life. Aristotle takes very seriously the "going" views about the human good and what appears choice-worthy to people. He acknowledges that there is at least some presumption in favor of beliefs that are widely held, supported by many people's experience, or maintained by those who are respected. He then goes on to submit those beliefs to critical examination in order to see if, indeed, they are what we should maintain. Aristotle's reasoning often leads him away from acceptance of those beliefs in the end, but this is how he generally finds his starting point. Even when he reaches conclusions very unlike his starting point, he arrives at the conclusion from an origin we can easily recognize; for example, things often said, what is widely held to be true, or perplexities that are widely felt. This is one type of philosophical method.

In *Meditations on First Philosophy,* Descartes proceeds in a very different manner. He says in the first meditation that if he is to "establish anything firm and lasting in the sciences"[1] he has to "raze everything to the ground."[2] He sought general reasons for doubting all of his former opinions, so that his mind would be clear of any preconceptions or prejudices. (Recall our discussion in chapter 2 of his "argument from dreaming.") Descartes held that in order to show that there are indeed adequate grounds for knowledge, we must suspend belief in anything we have accepted so far. This is part of his strategy of first formulating and then meeting and defeating the strongest possible skeptical challenge. He wanted to find out if there are any beliefs that are completely invulnerable to doubt. If, like Descartes, you believe that a very strong type of certainty is necessary for knowledge, then you must eliminate the most powerful grounds for doubt. Descartes rejects appearances and the way things seem, as a starting point in his investigation of knowledge.

Aristotle and Descartes not only have different views in the sense that lists of what they accept would include different entries, but the ways in which they proceed in philosophical argument and inquiry are quite different as well. The fact that in the *Ethics* Aristotle was writing about the nature of the good life, while in the *Meditations* Descartes was writing about the nature of knowledge (among other things), does not explain away the difference. There remains the contrast between a strategy that begins with widely held beliefs, examining them and revising them, and a strategy that begins by suspending all of our familiar beliefs and seeing if that leaves us with anything that is irresistible or certain. Aristotle and Descartes were both seeking first principles, but they went about the task in quite different ways. There is an important difference between arguing *from* first principles and arguing *to* them.

Further Exploration of Method

We will continue discussing philosophical strategy and the difference made by starting points. We do not have to go far to find the materials we need.

Right now, you are reading a book. Unless something quite out of the ordinary is going on, you have no special reason to doubt that you are looking at a book about philosophy and that it is in English, that it is larger than a postage stamp, that it cannot speak, walk, or turn over all by itself, and so forth. You might even wonder what sort of person *would* doubt any of those things. Why would you need to be *argued* into any of these beliefs? Why would they need to be *shown* to be true? You probably think that you can just see that they are true. Yet, what exactly *is* it that you are directly aware of? Is it the book, a perception of the book, or a group of discrete sense-impressions that the brain or the mind fashions into a single, unified visual experience? What is the relation of sense perception to belief? Do you *infer* that you see a book, or is there no reasoning involved in acquiring that belief? The issue of knowledge is a particularly effective one for exploring the significance of starting points and strategies of argument.

We saw that Descartes was not willing to use empirical evidence to support his claims and arguments. Approaching the issue quite differently, **G. E. Moore** (1873–1958) argued that we can *know* things that we cannot *prove*. For example, according to Moore, we can know that there are objects outside the mind and we can have conclusive reasons for believing this, even in the absence of proof of it. This is a crucial claim about the relationship between knowledge and proof.

One way to interpret Moore's argument is to see it this way: When asked whether we have knowledge of things outside the mind, we can answer by pointing out examples of that knowledge. Ask yourself, "Do I really know anything?" The answer might be, "Of course I do. I know I am reading a book." We do not have to first *prove* that knowledge is possible and then see if there are any actual cases of it. Rather, we can indicate what is plainly an instance of knowledge and then consider it carefully in order to see what makes it one. After all, if you are looking at the book before you (and you are, right?) *what else* could you appeal to in order to support the claim that you see a book before you? Is there something you could be more sure of that would justify you in your belief that you see a book before you?

You might try to find out as much as you can about the optics and physiology and brain science of visual perception, but that will not do the trick. After all, won't that just enlarge the number of empirical claims to be called into question in the same way? Are you not more sure ("Moore sure") that you see a book before you than you are sure that these scientific claims are true?

We will not try to settle any of these issues here. The point is to see that in developing a philosophical position, and in constructing a philosophical argument, it is not as though everyone starts in the same place, but they somehow come out with different results. If we ask, "What is the problem of knowledge?" we may simply have no idea how to proceed. Which problem? Why is knowledge problematic? What kind of knowledge? Perceptual knowledge? Mathematical knowledge? Knowledge of the past? All knowledge? A great deal of what is at stake is in the starting points, in the very formulation of the issues.

In "Epistemology Naturalized" the influential contemporary philosopher, **W. V. O. Quine** (1908–) writes: "The Cartesian quest for certainty had been the remote motivation of epistemology, both on its conceptual and its doctrinal side; but that quest was seen as a lost cause."[3] Quine argues that there is no *apriori* first philosophy (that is, philosophical theorizing prior to and independent of empirical inquiry) which supplies criteria for knowledge-claims. Rather, the methods of the sciences are validated or rationally justified in their own terms. His work on knowledge defends a version of **naturalism.** He wrote:

> The stimulation of his sensory receptors is all the evidence anybody has had to go on, ultimately, in arriving at his picture of the world. Why not just settle for psychology? Such a surrender of the epistemological burden to psychology is a move that was disallowed in earlier times as circular reasoning. If the epistemologist's goal is validation of the grounds of empirical science, he defeats his purpose by using psychology or other empirical science in the validation. However, such scruples against circularity have little point once we have stopped dreaming of deducing science from observations. If we are simply out to understand the relation between observation and science, we are well advised to use any available information, including that provided by the very science whose link with observation we are seeking to understand.[4]

This is part of Quine's project of showing how skeptical challenges to knowledge and the attempts to meet and defeat them are misplaced. He holds that the defense of knowledge-claims can be mounted in terms that come from the very sorts of inquiries about which we initially raised the skeptical questions. There is a way to show that the questions need not arise in the way that they are often thought to arise and with the force that they are typically understood to have. We do not need a justification of knowledge-claims at an intellectual Archimedean point from which we can achieve absolute philosophical certainty. The justification of scientific knowledge can be developed in scientific, naturalistic terms.

A quite different starting point is one that takes *language* to be the key to philosophical inquiry. According to this view, by looking at language in the right sorts of ways we can make progress with a number of long-standing philosophical issues. For example, in *The Idea of a Social Science,* **Peter Winch** (1926–1997) writes:

> To assume at the outset that one can make a sharp distinction between "the world" and "the language in which we try to describe the world," to the extent of saying that the problems of philosophy do not arise at all out of the former but only out of the latter, is to beg the whole question of philosophy.[5]

He argues that "in discussing language philosophically we are in fact discussing *what counts as belonging to the world.* Our idea of what belongs to the realm of reality is given for us in the language that we use. The concepts we have settle for us the form of the experience we have of the world."[6]

The focus on language has been prominent in philosophy during recent decades and is one of the most important developments in twentieth-century philosophy. According to many philosophers, that is the route that will take us furthest in successfully formulating and addressing philosophical issues

Let's take a quick panoramic view of the different strategies and starting points we have illustrated.

1. Moore held that there are things we can know without being able to prove that we know them. That sounds so *un*philosophical. Of course, Moore's point (whether he succeeded in making it or not) was that it was not at all unphilosophical. He was trying to show us that there are certain kinds of knowledge-claims that we have no reason to doubt and that it would be fruitless and beside the point to try to reason our way into accepting them.
2. Descartes' views emerge out of a rationalistic and realist approach.
3. Quine's views are part of a version of naturalism.
4. Winch's arguments are different in yet another way, emerging out of a linguistic approach. Where an argument leads depends crucially on where and how it began, and that is seldom a strictly logical matter. In settling upon a starting point and moving on from there, philosophical imagination and insight do some of their most important work. This is because your starting point is crucial for determining what kind of argumentative leverage you can exert.

Philosophical Method and Scientific Facts

We are in a good position now to look again at an issue we raised in chapter 1, namely, the relation of philosophy to the sciences and to facts, generally. This is an important issue because philosophical inquiry is often motivated by perplexities that arise in experience and in science, and sometimes we feel that what we now know in one or another science solves a philosophical problem. That may sometimes be true, but there is a danger in jumping too quickly to the conclusion that there are scientific solutions to philosophical problems. An illustration will help.

John Locke, like many other philosophers, made a distinction between **primary qualities** and **secondary qualities.** He described primary qualities as "utterly inseparable from the body, [any material object, not just a human body] in what estate soever it be."[7] The examples he gave are "solidity, extension, figure, and mobility."[8] An object, he thought, has primary qualities whether or not we perceive them, and we can sometimes perceive them in just the way in which they *are* qualities of objects. For example, a cannonball looks spherical because it is spherical. It resists us when we hold it in both hands and apply pressure to it because it really is a solid object. Secondary qualities, Locke said, are "qualities which in truth are nothing in the objects themselves but powers to produce various sensations in us by their primary qualities, i. e. by the bulk, figure, texture, and motion of their insensible parts, as colours, sounds, tastes, etc."[9]

The secondary qualities are not present in the object in just the way that we perceive them. Think, for example, of the sweetness of sugar. The sweet taste is not literally in the object in the way that it is perceived. There are real features of the object that cause us to experience the taste of it as sweet, but sweetness (as a quality of experience) is no more literally in the sugar than wakefulness is in a cup of strong coffee. Locke's point is that we often make the error of projecting a feature of some of our experiences onto things in the world, mistakenly regarding them as primary qualities.[10] Once we recognize the error, we can see both that there is this distinction between primary and secondary qualities, and that *the distinction can be drawn within sense experience.* We will see in a moment why this claim is so important.

Descartes also acknowledged a distinction between the features of objects in themselves and qualities that we attribute to objects on the basis of our perceptions of them. However, he made the distinction in a quite different way. He argued that we could know what are the most fundamental, essential features of physical objects on the basis of **innate** intellectual conceptions. Descartes thought that these features were known by reason, independent of sense perception. According to Descartes, the distinction between primary and secondary qualities depended upon the distinction between what was known by reason and what was perceived by the senses. The way he drew the line between primary and secondary qualities was quite different from the way Locke drew the line, and it is that difference which is philosophically important.

Descartes held that genuine science needed to be built on a foundation of innate ideas of reason. Only on that basis could we discover universal and certain truths about the essences of things. His position was that no knowledge of the existence and essence of things is possible without certainty, and no certainty is possible without innate ideas. Innate ideas, which are integral to the constitution of the mind and are not acquired in experience, are needed in order for us to have any knowledge at all, for they alone are immune to doubt. Locke believed that our knowledge does not extend to the real essences of things and that it is based upon the evidence of sense perception but is still genuine knowledge. The dispute over the distinction between primary and secondary qualities and how that distinction is made is a dispute about the nature and extent of knowledge, and that is why it is important. Locke and Descartes were not doing "armchair" natural science; they were doing philosophy.

They gave different interpretations of scientific knowledge because they argued from different starting points, indicative of their different views of the foundation and scope of knowledge. If we examine their claims as stand-alone factual claims, we may feel that we are in a position to dismiss the claims as false or scientifically backward. When we examine their claims as parts of overall views of the nature of knowledge and how it is possible, status and significance of the claims are both elevated. Instead of looking obsolete and incorrect, they begin to look important and instructive.

Recall our earlier discussions of realism and antirealism, essences and necessity, whether sense perception alone or reason alone is a faculty of knowledge, and the role of certainty in knowledge. These are all relevant to the distinction between primary and secondary qualities. What might initially look like an odd factual claim is actually an occasion for systematic philosophical inquiry. Even if the state of the sciences is much different today, there remain questions about:

1. What qualities are to be attributed to objects?
2. Can we have knowledge of the qualities of objects in their own right, not just in terms of how they are perceived by us?

> Do we perceive and know the world as it is in itself or only in ways that are shaped and limited by our minds and sense faculties?

It is Descartes' concern with certainty that seems to drive his philosophical method. He wanted to identify starting points immune to skeptical doubt, and he wanted to derive other claims from them by rigorous logic. Locke was not a less careful or rigorous thinker, but his conception of what is available as a starting point and his conception of the gravity of the skeptical challenge were quite different. It is with respect to that matter that we find some of the most important differences between them.

Understanding starting points is so important because it enables us to see that philosophical claims are not like ordinary empirical claims and that the appropriate methods of evaluating them are correspondingly different. If you are impressed by the Cartesian claim that a full-scale, global skeptical challenge must be met and defeated in order for us to make justified knowledge-claims, then it might seem to you that Locke, for example, is simply begging the crucial question. After all, if what we are inquiring into is the possibility of knowledge of objects outside the mind, surely we cannot start with the assumption that we have such knowledge and then just go on to make distinctions within it.

Locke, for his part, raised some important questions about what *sorts* of skeptical challenges we have the responsibility to answer and what resources we can deploy in answering them. Any position, except utter skeptical silence, will have to start with something. Even Descartes' theorizing did, in the respect that he insisted that he could safely accept ideas that he clearly and distinctly perceived, while he was perceiving them. (Descartes used the criteria of *clarity* and *distinctness* in a specific and centrally important way in the *Meditations.*) Locke maintained that we have no general, weighty reason to doubt that what seems to us to be sense perceptions of objects outside the mind really are perceptions of objects outside the mind. We do not need to be *reasoned* into a justified belief in the existence of objects outside the mind. Descartes maintained that we do indeed need an argument that proves that what we take to be perceptions of objects really are perceptions of objects. This illustrates how some of the most important differences in philosophical positions can be identified in terms of what needs to be established by argument.

Examples From Ethics

Other areas of philosophy also supply excellent examples of the significance of starting points and method. We can add texture to our discussion by looking at one of them—ethics. Aristotle, Immanuel Kant, and John Stuart Mill would show up on any list of influential ethical philosophers. The list could go deeper, but the inclusion of these three is uncontroversial. Let's briefly consider their approaches to ethics.

Aristotle's ethical philosophy is often referred to as a **virtue-theory,** Kant's as a **deontological** theory, and Mill's as a **consequentialist** theory. We will say a bit about what those terms mean shortly, but right now, the point is that it would be a misconception to think that you can just opt for one approach rather than another. These (like realism and antirealism) are not like menu items. Endorsement of one or another of these approaches should be based on other things you believe—for example, what you believe about the nature of human motivation and about what human beings fundamentally *are.* A conception of ethical requirements will be embedded in views about those things. In studying the works of great ethical theorists, we are not just examining their views about moral obligation or about what is morally permissible or impermissible, we are studying different conceptions of human nature and how moral value figures in a human life.

Mill, for example, argues that "pleasure and freedom from pain are the only things desirable as ends; and that all desirable things (which are as numerous in the utilitarian as in any other scheme) are desirable either for pleasure inherent in themselves or as means to the promotion of pleasure and the prevention of pain."[11] His view of the fundamental nature of human beings is that they are pleasure-seeking creatures. Mill's theory of value is a type of **hedonism** because he takes pleasure to be good, to be what is intrinsically valuable, but he is not a vulgar hedonist. Mill's view is *not* that people should pursue whatever pleases them. He argues that there are superior and inferior pleasures and that it is important that people should be educated and encouraged to pursue superior pleasures. Still, his moral theory is based upon a conception of human nature according to which our capacity to experience pleasure and pain is fundamental.

On that basis Mill argues that the criterion of morally right action is such that:

> actions are right in proportion as they tend to promote happiness; wrong as they tend to produce the reverse of happiness. By happiness is

> intended pleasure and the absence of pain; by unhappiness, pain and the privation of pleasure.[12]

This type of moral theory is **utilitarianism.** In this view, the most basic and general moral requirement is to impartially promote utility or happiness. This is the basis for evaluating actions. We are to look at what difference actions make and what they bring about, with reference to happiness and misery. It is a consequentialist theory because actions are evaluated on the basis of their expected consequences rather than their motives. Is the act expected to make people better off or worse off? Would a different action have a greater probability of producing much greater gains in utility without causing suffering? According to this view, acts are not themselves right or wrong, but are evaluated on account of what differences they are expected to make.

Our main concern is to point out how Mill's proposed criterion of right action, his proposed fundamental principle of moral obligation, is grounded on a conception of human nature. If hedonistic utilitarianism makes sense and is defensible, it will be because this sort of conception of human nature and intrinsic value supports it. For Mill, the debate about what has intrinsic value is settled by an examination of facts about human nature. In particular, it is settled by facts about desire and what is desired for its own sake. He maintains that the evidence needed to support his theory is available through observation and the empirical sciences. This is a version of ethical naturalism.

Kant has a very different moral theory, and this is largely because his conception of human nature is different. Kant argues that it is the fact that we are rational beings that is crucial to the understanding of morality. He and Mill give quite different answers to the question, "What is it about human beings that makes them participants in a moral order?" (I do not mean that they explicitly asked this question, but that it is plainly one of their basic concerns.)

For Mill, what matters is the fact that we experience pleasure and pain. Pleasure is better than pain. Pleasure is desired for its own sake. Therefore, the rational and moral thing to do is to impartially promote pleasure. For Kant, what matters most is that we are capable of acting on rational principles. He argues that everyone in their own experience as agents can distinguish between obligation and inclination. Each of us can recognize the difference between doing something because of our desires or passions and doing something because it is right. Of course people want to be happy, and it is rational to pursue happiness. Nonetheless, the only thing that has unqualified, unconditional value is the good will. Kant says, "It need hardly be mentioned that the sight of a being adorned with no feature of a pure and good will, yet enjoying uninterrupted prosperity, can never give pleasure to a rational impartial observer. Thus the good will seems to constitute the indispensable condition even of worthiness to be happy."[13] By "good will" Kant does not mean feelings for our fellow men or compassion for others. A rational agent's will is good when that agent acts on right principles because they are right principles. These are principles that could be endorsed by any impartial rational agent, independently of each agent's desires and subjective interests.

Kant's ethical theory is an example of a deontological theory, which is a theory of duties that we have because of certain types of action being intrinsically right and others being intrinsically wrong. For Mill, the consequentialist, types of action are not right or wrong in themselves but on account of what they are expected to bring about.

Each theory plausibly pulls us in a different direction. Most of us probably believe that there are some types of actions that are intrinsically wrong. We might think that even if they did someone some good or even if they made people happier, they would still be wrong. We sometimes think, "It is not a matter of how much good it brings about; if it's wrong, it's wrong." We can imagine taking this view about the making of deceitful promises. There may be occasions on which deceitful promises would make many people better off; but it is still wrong to make them, and their intrinsic wrongness is an adequate reason not to make them. Often, however, it also seems to us that consequences matter and that they are sometimes decisive. We might find ourselves arguing like this: "I know that doing this seems wrong, but surely you see that it is better overall that we should go ahead with it." We might say this about certain kinds of experimental testing of new drugs on patients who are not aware of the tests. (It is important to see that the utilitarian is *not* saying that we can be justified in doing something that is wrong if the good that we expect it to bring about is significant. Rather, the utilitarian argues that we should stop thinking in terms of actions as intrinsically right or wrong. Instead, we should ascertain their rightness or wrongness in terms of their utility. So if an act has a great deal of utility, then it is not a wrong act but still somehow permissible. It is a right act.)

Both Kant and Mill claim to be seeking the fundamental criterion or principle of right action, and they each claim to be supplying an account of what people already implicitly recognize as the principle of morals. They do not see themselves as drastically revising people's moral convictions. Rather, they see themselves as articulating and justifying what is correct in what people already believe. They cannot both be entirely right because their views are opposed in so many ways. Yet, it is possible that each of them is recognizing important features of moral experience and our conceptions of human nature. Pleasure and happiness are important to us, and consideration of them figures prominently in our decisions about what is good and about how to act. We *are* creatures of sensibility. At the same time, we are also rational creatures, and it is important to us that we acknowledge and respect each other as rational agents capable of acting on principles. The differences between Mill and Kant are deep differences in the sense that their moral theories not only articulate conceptions of what we ought to do and why, but they are embedded in conceptions of what we most fundamentally *are.*

Aristotle's ethical theorizing is different in yet another way. His main concern is not to identify a fundamental criterion or principle of right action but to articulate a conception of *human flourishing,* a conception of what is the best kind of life for a human being. The points we earlier made about Aristotle's method apply here. He begins by taking seriously the most widely held views of the matter. It is as though he is asking the question, "How should one live?" rather than the question, "What are my moral duties?" There is a difference between a concern with what are our obligations and a concern with what sort of person to become and what sort of life is the best life. Aristotle formulates and addresses the fundamental questions of value differently from Kant and Mill in this way, and this difference is intimately connected with his conception of human nature.

For Aristotle, it is crucial to understand the distinctively human *virtues.* This is the issue of what characteristics are needed by a person in order to be an excellent person and to lead an excellent life. Aristotle's concern is with what sort of enduring characteristics we need, and what sorts of things we should value, in order to lead a life that is found to be worthwhile and pleasing in itself by the person who leads it. This is not an account of how to maximize pleasure. It is an account of how a human being can most successfully actualize distinctively human potentialities.

Aristotle believed that there was a crucial connection between virtue and happiness. He held that virtuous activity is pleasing to the agent who engages in it. It is pleasing in part because that agent appreciates the excellence of his activity. The agent's happiness is merited on account of his virtue. This is not a sort of conceit or arrogance. Rather, Aristotle was making the point that *being* good *is* a good; the excellent agent is not wracked by internal conflict, remorse, or regret.

The virtuous person can truly judge his life and his character to be desirable and worthy and finds this pleasing.

Aristotle, Kant, and Mill each claim to be presenting accounts of *objective* ethical considerations, but their notions of the ways in which they are objective are quite different. For Mill, the objectivity of ethical considerations is empirical, factual objectivity. He maintains that ethical judgments can be put on a broadly scientific basis. It is, he believed, a calculable matter of fact that one course of action can be expected to promote utility better than another. For Kant, the objectivity of ethical considerations is the objectivity of universal rational principles. He maintains that the test of universalization is a criterion independent of empirical considerations. The objectivity of the criterion of right action, according to Kant, is the objectivity of rational necessity. Aristotle argues that there are objective goods for human beings, given the fundamental capacities of human nature, and what it is for their exercise to be well-ordered. He understands ethical objectivity in terms of the distinctive and proper function of a human being. Clearly, even among those who agree that ethical considerations are objective, there are deep and important differences over how objectivity is to be interpreted.

When we study Kant or Mill, Plato or Aristotle, Hume or any other of the great moral philosophers, we are also exploring what it is to be a human being. We are exploring issues concerning the nature of value and the nature of motivation and what unites us in a common moral world. These authors are not self-appointed moral maestros, telling us what we should do. They are inviting us to consider looking at the most basic questions about value in certain ways.

The ethical context is one in which the value of studying philosophy is especially evident. We often find that people disagree about ethical matters and sometimes these disagreements are quite heated. Arguments about health care, affirmative action, gun control, and countless other issues occur all the time outside of philosophy classes. That is one of the main reasons why philosophy classes are valuable. Using philosophical skills to address the issues is not a way of removing them from "real life" and making them academic issues. It is a very effective way of making progress with real life concerns and disputes by being able to identify more sharply just what is at issue and by addressing the issue with argumentation based upon reason. Sometimes just clarifying the ways in which certain terms are used or clarifying the basic structure of an argument can go a long way in reducing the tension in a disagreement, and that is the kind of skill which becomes "second nature" in doing philosophy.

The Explanation of Human Action

We are going to turn our attention now to an area of philosophy about which you almost certainly have some views of your own. This is the free will and **determinism** debate. It, too, is fertile ground for exploring claims about the importance of starting points and differences in method.

One of the fundamental approaches to explaining human action is determinism. Determinism has been defined in a number of different ways, but the basic idea of determinism is that a human action, like any other event, is brought about by causes. That is to say, all human actions are causally necessitated. How else could it be? The determinist maintains that even when we are doing what we want, and nothing is forcing us to act, our actions are caused because our desires, beliefs, feelings, and so forth are among the causes of our actions. Our actions do not randomly or mysteriously come from nowhere. The notion that whatever happens has been caused to happen seems so natural and so basic, that it is not surprising that it should also apply to human actions.

Some theorists who accept determinism also argue that because determinism is true, people are not morally responsible for their actions. They argue that if our actions are causally necessitated, they are unavoidable, and if they are unavoidable, then we cannot do otherwise than what we in fact do. Therefore, we are not morally responsible. This does not mean that now we can just go ahead and do awful things and no one will care. This is a point about the implications of determinism and about how to interpret and justify matters such as blame and punishment. That interpretation of determinism is often called **hard determinism.**

Libertarianism is the view that human beings have free will in the sense that at least some of our actions are not causally necessitated, but these actions are not just random either. Determinists often argue that if there were not sufficient causes for actions, they would be random or chance events; either they are caused or no one could know why they happen. The libertarian argues that there is another alternative. An act can be a free and meaningful act of an agent (not just a random event) though it is *not* causally necessitated. There is a way to understand a free action as being the act of an agent (and not something that just happens) without interpreting it as causally necessitated.

The first point to note is that the libertarian claims that determinism is false.[14] So, according to the libertarian, it is false that everything that happens is causally necessitated (even if most things are). The libertarian need not argue that *no* events are causally necessitated. In fact, that would be immensely implausible. What must be true for libertarianism to be true is that at least *some* human actions are not causally necessitated, and human beings have free will in the sense that we are agents who can act freely. According to the libertarian, we can only be morally responsible for acts we perform freely, and we do indeed perform some such acts.

Another position maintains that causal necessity is in fact compatible with moral responsibility. This view may or may not assert that determinism is true, though it maintains that the truth of it would not be incompatible with moral responsibility. According to this view, when it is your own character or choice that is the cause of an act, that makes the act voluntary and your own, and you are responsible for it. The claim is that there is an important difference between the case in which the cause of an action is your own wants and beliefs and the case in which the cause is a compulsion or an external force. The fact that an act is caused does not render it unfree. It depends what kind of cause the act has. This view is often called **compatibilism.**

There are different versions of compatibilism. Some compatibilists argue that *even if* our actions are caused, those with certain types of causes are free actions and we are responsible for them. Other compatibilists argue that determinism *is* true and it is compatible with free will and moral responsibility. Still other compatibilists argue that determinism is true, and *only if* determinism is true can we perform actions for which we are morally responsible. If there were no way to causally trace actions to our beliefs, desires, intentions, and character, what basis would we have for thinking that they are our actions? These latter two versions of compatibilism are sometimes called **soft determinism** because they include the claim that determinism (at least with regard to human action) is true.

Here again, it is not only the formal structure and validity of the arguments that matter. After all, the libertarian and the hard determinist can agree that *if* our actions are causally necessitated, then we are not morally responsible for them. They disagree over whether to accept the "if" clause. What grounds are there to believe that indeed our actions are caused or that they are not caused? If they are not caused, how are we to explicate the respect in which they are free? The libertarian is not just insisting that some actions are not causally necessitated but also that they are *free* actions in a way such that the agents who perform them are morally responsible for them. Random or capricious actions without some grounding in the agent's controlling conceptions of what he or she is doing and why, would not be free actions. Determinists will try to show that random or capricious action is the only alternative to determinism, and thus the libertarian is trapped in a dilemma fatal to his position. Either actions are causally necessitated, or they are random, and in neither case can they be free in the libertarian's sense. Determinists insist that any meaningful connection to the agent's character, deliberations, or choices is a causal connection.

What might motivate someone to adopt one of these positions over one of the others? Many people are impressed by advances in scientific explanation, and noting that much of science arrives at causal explanations, they may be motivated by this to embrace determinism. One way in which this might happen is as follows: "While it is true that we do not currently possess complete and accurate causal explanations of human behavior, it is reasonable to believe that, in principle, there are such explanations. Human beings and their behavior are exceedingly complex, but they are not so different in kind from the rest of the world that we should think of them as not being fully subject to the laws of nature. Where we have not yet found causes, it makes sense to look for them. To say that human actions are caused is not to say that people are helpless puppets or robots or are subject to constant coercion. It just means that there are causes for their actions."

Remember, some determinists are soft determinists, and they maintain that the truth of determinism does not mean that people do not or cannot act voluntarily and are not responsible for their actions.

The idea here is that the behavior of human beings can be conceptualized and explained in terms of the same categories and general methods that we use to causally explain other parts of nature. Determinism, it is often argued, is the scientific, objective stand on this matter. Determinists sometimes explicitly point this out, and they note that libertarian arguments often seem unscientific or that they seem to be motivated by religious or moral considerations that have no privileged place in the explanation of action.

Libertarians sometimes argue that each one of us knows, on the basis of our own experience, that some of our actions are literally "up to" us. There is a kind of practical self-knowledge, an awareness of ourselves as free agents, that gives conclusive evidence that determinism is false. When we deliberate, we decide on the basis of how we weigh considerations and how we give thought to the question of how to act. The resulting action is a free action, not an act that is causally necessitated or made unavoidable by antecedent events. Some theorists have argued that we know we are free because we can sometimes act contrary to our strongest desires when they conflict with what we believe we *ought* to do.

The free will versus determinism debate is a particularly effective issue for illustrating the interconnectedness of philosophical problems. It also illustrates the way in which what looks like a debate going on at one level actually has roots that go deep and branches that go wide in ways that we do not notice when we first become acquainted with it. It is a debate about how best to conceptualize human nature and human behavior. Should our nature and our behavior be understood along the lines that have proved so fruitful in the natural sciences? Is there a distinctively humanistic way to understand human behavior? What is the best account of how human actions fit into the larger natural order?

One of the most important and controversial aspects of the debate about freedom of will is whether there is only one type of causality or more than one. Determinists tend to argue that there is one type. We shall call it **event-causality,** according to which causation is a relation between events, and there is nothing special about human actions in respect to their causes. Determinists may disagree among themselves over just what are the main causal processes and mechanisms of human action. There may be genetic, physical, psychological, social, and other kinds of causes operating in complex interaction. The bottom line, though, for determinists is that causation is causation—a certain kind of relation between events. Whatever kinds of events turn out to be the causally relevant ones, determinists will generally agree that the type of causation that is involved in human action (event-causation) is not distinctive.

Libertarians often argue that, in addition to the causation of events by other events, there is **agent-causality.** This is the power by which a being (in this case a human being) can initiate action, can do something, without being caused to do so by any prior events. Part of what is at issue between the libertarian and the determinist is the question of just what a human action is. If, as the libertarian argues, we sometimes act knowingly and voluntarily without there being any events that causally necessitate us to act in those ways, then in those instances we act freely, and we are responsible for our actions.

This is not to say that libertarians believe that human actions come from nowhere or that a person can do just anything. We cannot, for example, leap tall buildings in a single bound (like Superman), nor can we eat if there is no food available. We cannot put out a fire just by looking at it or be sitting on the Great Wall of China two seconds from now, if we are not in China. There are many things we simply are unable to do, and there are many conditions that must be fulfilled for us to do any of the things that we are able to do. Maybe you have the strength to freely throw a three-pound metal ball more than fifty feet. Still, many physical conditions over which you have little control must exist in order for you to actually be able to do that.

Thus, there is an important difference between the causally **necessary conditions** for an action and causally **sufficient conditions.** The libertarian will argue that *of course* there are necessary conditions, even for free acts, but there are not causally sufficient conditions. If there were, the acts would not be free acts. Sufficient conditions would be enough to cause the act. There can, though, be necessary conditions in place without being sufficient conditions.[15] For example, if you are to freely get up and leave the room, you must be alive, able to move about, there must be a way out of the room, and so forth. Maybe you will just decide to stay put. Nothing is keeping you there against your will. Nothing is compelling you to leave. The libertarian says that you are staying in the room on account of your own free agency.

Determinists insist that agent-causality is mysterious or just plain incoherent. They argue that this additional category of causality is simply not needed; we can explain all that we need to about human actions in terms of event-causality. Anyway, how could anything initiate action by literally starting a completely new chain of causation? Surely, everything that happens is itself caused by something else. Libertarians respond that, of course, we know the difference between being caused to act and acting freely through an exercise of agency. Why should we reject the evidence of our own awareness of ourselves as agents, only to save a theory? After all, does anyone *know* that determinism is true? In fact, how *could* someone know that it is true? If it is an empirical thesis, surely we lack the vast amount of evidence that would be needed to support it. Is it then a necessary truth, and is it known *apriori?* It seems not to be. What contradiction or inconsistency is there in the notion of an event or an action that is not sufficiently caused? It is true that to search for causes in trying to explain things is a very reasonable thing to do, and it often yields true explanations. Is that enough to conclude that all human actions are causally necessitated?

What is at stake in this debate is what we might call the *interpretation* of human action. What is the most plausible conception or the most illuminating understanding of human action? Should we seek to explain human action in the ways that we explain other kinds of events? What is the relevant type of data or evidence for an account of human action? What account of human action fits best with other beliefs that we have about such things as morality, rationality, and self-knowledge?

A Culminating Case Study

By looking at one very influential general philosophical outlook we can illustrate many of the general themes we have discussed so far. This outlook is **naturalism**. It is a view with many contemporary adherents, and there are naturalist positions in ethics, in epistemology, in philosophy of mind, and in other areas of philosophy. It supplies a good case study of our claims about the importance of starting points, differences in method, and the relation of philosophy to science.

There are many different versions of naturalism. What is common to them is this: With respect to what is philosophically at issue, (whether it is moral value, knowledge, human action, the relation of mind and body, etc.) the subject can be explained by the methods of the natural sciences. The methods of the sciences give us access to whatever is needed to understand what is philosophically problematic.

For example, Mill's utilitarian theory is an example of ethical naturalism. He argued that moral value can be understood in terms of desire and pleasure. Pleasure is what is desired for its own sake, and not for the sake of anything else; thus, it is good for its own sake (and not merely good as a means to something else). There is nothing mysterious or deeply metaphysical about moral value. It can be fully understood in terms of natural facts about the psychology of desire and pleasure. Moral judgments are objective, factual judgments about the extent to which utility is increased or diminished.

Quine's position in epistemology is another example of naturalism. He argues that the methods of science can be self-correcting and can be validated in their own terms. They do not need a foundation supplied from any standpoint external to them. This is why he thinks the Cartesian project of trying to find special, philosophically certain foundations for science is both unnecessary and doomed to fail. The methods of science can validate the methods of science. This is not a vicious circle because the very nature of the scientific method demands rigorous tests and observational data. Our successes at scientific explanation are evidence that indeed, those methods are valid. According to Quine's view, the distinctively philosophical project concerned with the defeat of skepticism should be abandoned in favor of sciences that will disclose the causal process of belief-formation and acceptance and the like. That is one important version of epistemological naturalism.

The naturalist in philosophy of mind typically argues that mental states and thought processes can be explained in terms of biology, physics, and chemistry. Naturalism rejects the claim that a mind is a substance or entity that is distinct from the body and that possesses its own distinct powers. Consciousness, cognitive processes, the emotions, memory, and so forth, are all to be understood and explained in terms of physical entities and processes. The laws discovered by the sciences apply no less fully to the mind than to the body. Here, as in the other areas we have mentioned, the naturalist seeks to assimilate or "domesticate" an area of philosophical investigation into the sciences.

It is not surprising that naturalism should have great appeal. For one thing, it seems to be a strategy that demystifies issues and makes them more tractable. We can tell when we are making progress with naturalistic explanations. Also, it puts a restraint on speculative excesses. The naturalist insists that hypotheses and explanations must survive the rigors of scientific testing. The enormous successes of the sciences give many people confidence that the employment and continual correction of scientific methods will enable us to solve problems that seemed unique to philosophy. At the very least, we will be able to see the limits of our ability to solve those problems.

Keep in mind, though, that naturalism is *itself* a philosophical position. It is a view of what counts as an adequate explanation, genuine knowledge, and what kinds of things reality includes. It is an excellent illustration of something we said earlier: That there is always a philosophical dimension to science, however advanced it is. Whether or not naturalism is true is a philosophical question, and it invites a philosophical answer, arrived at by ongoing reflection. There is no doubt that the sciences demand high levels of intellectual responsibility, precision, and rigor. It is still a *philosophical* issue whether the methods and practice of science are the whole story with regard to what there is, what things are like, and to what extent they are knowable. The genuineness and the normativity of philosophy are not eliminated by naturalism.

Positions and Traditions

Naturalism has been especially influential recently in philosophy because of the impressive advances in the sciences. It is not, however, a position that has appeared on the landscape only recently. Its current forms have ancient ancestors. In that sense, we can say that there has long been a naturalist tradition. It is likely that you will encounter many different traditions in your study of philosophy, and the more widely you study, the more clearly they will come into view. We should comment briefly on the significance of recognizing traditions in philosophy.

Different positions, even positions which are opposed in many ways, can belong to the same tradition. There is a sense in which both Descartes (a rationalist) and Hume (an empiricist) can be said to belong to the modern tradition, in contrast to, for example, the medieval scholastic tradition. This is not simply a matter of chronology. What locates Descartes and Hume in the modern tradition has to do with how they see the project of philosophy and not just what time period they lived in.

There are different ways of identifying traditions, and they do not come to us in neat, distinct packages. Instead of trying to strictly define what is meant by "tradition," it is probably best to just mention a few traditions. It is very likely that you will hear about or see references to the "analytic tradition," the "continental tradition," the "modern tradition," the "scholastic tradition," the "rationalist tradition," the "existentialist tradition," and perhaps others as well. There is a fairly clear sense in which these names refer to different traditions if by "tradition" we mean something like a body of central texts, a set of central problems, and certain distinctive ways of approaching those problems.

In that sense, philosophers such as A. J. Ayer and W. V. O. Quine belong to the analytic tradition, while **Martin Heidegger** (1889–1976) and **Jean-Paul Sartre** (1905–1980) belong to the continental tradition (and to the existentialist tradition, in particular). When you read authors in different traditions, you will notice that they sometimes use philosophical vocabulary differently and they sometimes also use different philosophical vocabulary. You will see that their methods and the sorts of evidence that they appeal to are different. It can sometimes seem that they are inhabiting quite different intellectual "worlds" and that they share very little.

To some extent, that must be admitted. There are real and substantial differences. The differences, though, can be overplayed, and overplaying them has its dangers. It can politicize philosophy, dividing it into camps or parties. Once party loyalty becomes an issue there is the risk of dogmatism, dismissal of the work of the other party, and a whole host of other vices that come with division along party lines. To judge the work of another tradition dismissively, as "oh, *that* stuff" is about as unphilosophical as you can get.

You may find that a certain tradition formulates the problems of philosophy in a way that seems to you to be the deepest and most compelling. To your mind, those philosophers are worried about the right things, and they approach them in what seem to you to be the right ways. Almost everyone who pursues the study of philosophy does settle into a certain philosophical stance or perspective. Some see themselves as basically Kantian, or basically Humean, or basically **analytic,** or **existentialist** in their approach, for example. It is good to have a philosophical "home base," a place from which to conduct your explorations, a center of philosophical gravity, as it were. It is also important not to let that harden into a defensive or dogmatic stance. Again, that would be unphilosophical.

You can learn a great deal from those outside of the tradition in which you locate yourself. Indeed, the process of settling into certain positions may take place as a result of reading and studying widely, and exploring the rich plurality of views, arguments, and methods. Your judgment that, say, libertarianism is the most plausible position with regard to human action, should be reinforced by a critical appreciation of hard determinism and compatibilism. Similarly, your larger philosophical commitments should also be based on wide critical awareness. A closer look reveals that many of the problems taken up by the different traditions are very much the same and that there are commonalities of concern that are not visible directly on the surface. For example, questions about the relation of language to the world and about the role of conceptualization in constituting objects are shared by analytic philosophers and philosophers in the continental tradition.

The different traditions are not wholly isolated from each other. While it can be helpful to recognize philosophers as belonging to one or another tradition, the divisions between the traditions can be easily overstated. Often, philosophers who see themselves as working in one tradition have been influenced by other traditions simply because the people whose work they study most and respect most have almost certainly learned from, borrowed from, and responded to philosophers in other traditions.

There are very great philosophers, such as Plato and Aristotle, who have had enormous influence of different kinds and who have been important to a number of different traditions. Their depth and importance are inexhaustible and continue to figure in even the most contemporary work in many different ways. Truly great philosophy is like that. It is not that Aristotle, for example, has "followers" who are Aristotelians in some orthodox doctrinal way, but that his insights and arguments remain relevant to the project of philosophy. We are not just learning *about* his philosophy, we are still learning *from* it—and from Plato's, Hume's, Kant's, and others'.

It is unfortunate that philosophy is sometimes undertaken in an adversarial way, pitting one tradition against others. That is a distraction from the main work of philosophy. "Hear the truth from whoever says it"[16] says the medieval Jewish philosopher **Maimonides** (1135–1204). It is sound advice.

No doubt there are times when one feels that a certain tradition has just got it all wrong or that a certain formulation of an issue is the right one and others are confused. When that really is how it seems to you, by all means say so and give the reasons why. If there are reasons, then it is not just party rhetoric, and your participation in the debate is genuine. To some extent, it can be a good thing to see yourself as a thinker in a certain tradition. As we noted, it gives you a home base, an orientation that can surely be revised and adjusted, but which also sets you on your way. We should, however, carefully guard against becoming complacent or too comfortable with that orientation. When our thinking ceases to be relentless, it ceases to be genuine philosophical thought.

Being a Kantian, an Aristotelian, a Sartrean, or any other philosophical "ian" should not mean that you just say what that philosopher said or that you have a fixed way of answering philosophical questions. It should mean that you value the resources in someone's thought in such a way that you believe that the persistent problems of philosophy can be constructively addressed by the development of these resources. In a sense, you *cannot* just say what that philosopher said because the problems are still real and they demand continuing, renewed attention. It is better to work on the problem that concerns you than to just adopt what you take to be someone's view of it. The reason for being a philosophical "ian" is that the issues have not been finally and conclusively resolved, though you think there are special merits in approaching them in certain ways.

Your first exposure to philosophy can have a very powerful formative influence. Almost everyone who goes on to further study will admit this. If it is, for example, the existentialists who fire your imagination and bring philosophy to life for you right at the start, that influence may continue to make a great deal of difference in your thinking. Perhaps a teacher has handled certain texts and topics in such a way that you develop an appetite for more and begin to feel that the study of philosophy or works of philosophy is important to you. Aristotle remarks that "no equivalent honour can be paid"[17] to those "who have shared philosophy in common with us. For its worth is not measured in money. . . ."[18] If you are very fortunate, you will have the sort of learning experience that will enable you to agree.

Whatever tradition, approach, text, or author most shapes your early views of philosophy, it is healthy to have the willingness and ambition to explore others. Even if your philosophical center of gravity does not shift, you will at least have an enlarged awareness of how issues are seen and a deepened understanding of the views you endorse, on account of exposure to alternatives to and criticisms of them.

Where We Are Now

Several of our themes are illustrated by the debates about epistemology, ethics, and human action.

1. Philosophical problems can be motivated by reflection on quite familiar issues and experiences.
2. The problems are often connected in important, even if not obvious, ways.
3. The precise use of language is crucial in philosophical inquiry and argument.
4. Your starting point can make an important difference to your formulation of an issue and approach to it.
5. There are differences in philosophical methods and corresponding differences in the sorts of evidence that these methods use. There are also differences in the understanding of the most serious objections.

By now you should have a working conception of many of the features of philosophical problems, and you should be better able to notice the ways in which they are common across different contexts. Also, you should be attuned to the ways in which a stand on one issue has connections to other issues and implications for them.

In our observations about traditions, we emphasized the importance of remaining open to different ways of approaching philosophical problems. Seeing yourself as heir to a tradition or acknowledging the appeal of a tradition can helpfully shape and direct your thinking. It is a way of achieving a large-scale perspective. At the same time, it is contrary to the spirit of philosophy to regard a tradition as making no contribution to the philosophical project or as leaving no room for the contributions of others.

In the final chapter we will look closely at some important aspects of writing philosophy papers. We noted at the outset that philosophy both demands and strengthens a broad range of abilities. The clearest evidence of this is when you have to commit your thoughts to paper. It is in writing that you really find out how fully you understand and appreciate the texts and topics you have been thinking about. Writing is also a way to refine, organize, and elaborate your thinking. It can be an important part of getting "inside" philosophy and finding your way about rather than looking at it from a distance.

Some Things to Think About and Discuss

1. Consider the following line of reasoning: "The combination of social surroundings and natural temperament determine a person's character. If people ever act freely it is only in the sense that they are not coerced or compelled, but they are not responsible for their characters. Therefore, they should not be held morally responsible for their actions, because actions are just expressions of character." Is that a good argument to show that people are not responsible for their characters and do not act freely? Does it seem to you that people ever act in ways that are "out of character"? If they do, what is the significance of that fact for the debate about free will?
2. Suppose your instructor announces early in the term that no one in the course will receive a grade lower than B. If you work hard and earn a B, you will get a B. If you never come to class and do poorly on exams and papers, or do not complete them, you will receive a B. You can earn grades higher than B, but B is the lowest grade anyone will receive. Are there utilitarian reasons in favor of this policy? Are there utilitarian reasons against it? What other kinds of ethical considerations are there in favor of it or against it?
3. Every philosopher has to have a starting point. Consider a fundamental philosophical issue, such as freedom of the will, the existence of God, or the possibility of knowledge. What do

you "take for granted" as a starting point on that issue? Why *that* starting point rather than a different one? Can you think of reasons that call into question your starting point? What do you find questionable about other starting points on the issue? Can you show that assumptions different from your own are mistaken?

Key Philosophers and Texts

Thomas Aquinas (1225–1274) *Summa Theologica:* Aquinas is a key figure in the medieval scholastic tradition. He sought to articulate and defend Christian theological doctrine with resources found in Aristotle's philosophy. This is a classic work in which faith and reason are reconciled.

Aristotle (384–322 B.C.) *Nicomachean Ethics, Metaphysics, Physics:* Aristotle's works have been, and remain, significant in all areas of philosophy. His defense of essentialism and his virtue-centered ethical theory are two of his most important contributions. He was also the first to develop a theory of logic in a systematic way.

A. J. Ayer (1910–1989) *Language, Truth, and Logic:* Ayer is a key figure in twentieth-century empiricism, and he presented an influential critique of ethical objectivity.

René Descartes (1596–1650) *Meditations on First Philosophy:* This work remains a classic of epistemology and metaphysics and is a crucial formulation of the skeptical challenge and the attempt to meet it and defeat it.

Martin Heidegger (1889–1976) *Being and Time:* This is a landmark work of twentieth-century existentialism.

David Hume (1711–1776) *An Enquiry Concerning Human Understanding, An Enquiry Concerning the Principles of Morals:* Hume's antirealist interpretation of morality remains a key source in the debates about whether there are objective values and the roles of reason and passion in moral motivation.

Immanuel Kant (1732–1804) *Foundations of the Metaphysics of Morals:* This remains the most important presentation of a deontological ethical theory.

John Locke (1632–1704) *An Essay Concerning Human Understanding:* This is a key work of modern philosophy and, in particular, of the British empiricist tradition.

Maimonides (1135–1204) "Eight Chapters": Maimonides was a medieval Jewish theologian and philosopher who sought to articulate and defend Jewish religion with the resources of Aristotle's philosophy. There are also some Platonic elements to his thought.

G. E. Moore (1873–1958) "A Defense of Common Sense," "Proof of an External World": Moore's analytic methods and his critique of skepticism were major influences on twentieth-century Anglo-American philosophy.

Plato (429–347 B.C.) *Republic, Apology, Phaedo:* Plato's dialogues remain classics of philosophical thought and literary quality. His explorations of justice, ethical value, and the nature of the self are still works of the first importance.

W. V. O. Quine (1908–) "Epistemology Naturalized": Quine is an important defender of naturalism. His work has been very influential in philosophy of language and epistemology.

Thomas Reid (1710–1796) *Essays on the Intellectual Powers of Man, An Inquiry:* Reid was a critic of both the rationalism and empiricism of his day, and he argued that both made assumptions that led to skeptical conclusions. He is also a defender of agent-causality.

Jean-Paul Sartre (1905–1980) *Being and Nothingness:* Sartre is a major existentialist philosopher and literary figure, important both in Europe and in English-language philosophy.

Socrates (c. 470–399 B.C.) Socrates left no writings, but he formulated many key philosophical problems, and his views are presented and developed by Plato in many of Plato's dialogues.

Peter Winch (1926–1997) *The Idea of a Social Science:* Winch was an important interpreter of Wittgenstein, and in this book he argues that the methods of the social sciences are fundamentally different from the methods of the natural sciences. We must, he argues, look at social behavior and institutions through an understanding of the language and practices of those we study, rather than trying to discover causal laws governing their behavior.

Ludwig Wittgenstein (1889–1951) *Philosophical Investigations, On Certainty:* Wittgenstein's works led philosophers to some quite dramatic reconsiderations of the relations between thought, language, and reality. He has influenced the work being done in many areas of philosophy and his work has been interpreted in many quite different ways. His examination of knowledge-claims led to some important reevaluations of skepticism and whether it is the sort of fundamental concern that many philosophers have taken it to be.

Endnotes

1. René Descartes, *Meditations on First Philosophy*, ed. Donald A. Cress, 3rd ed., (Indianapolis: Hackett Publishing Company, 1993), p. 13.
2. Ibid., p. 13.
3. W. V. O. Quine, "Epistemology Naturalized," in *Ontological Relativity and Other Essays* (New York: Columbia University Press, 1969), p. 74.
4. Ibid., pp. 75–76.
5. Peter Winch, *The Idea of a Social Science*, 2nd ed., (Atlantic Highlands: Humanities Press International, Inc., 1990), p. 18.
6. Ibid., p. 15.
7. John Locke, *An Essay Concerning Human Understanding*, ed. A. D. Woozley (New York: New American Library, Penguin Books USA, 1974), p. 112.
8. Ibid., p. 112.
9. Ibid., p. 112.
10. This is an important point in other contexts as well. For example, it has been argued that a similar projective error is made when people claim that moral values are objective. The idea is that we project feelings of approval onto things, thinking of them as objectively good, and we project our disapproval, thinking of things as objectively bad.
11. John Stuart Mill, *Utilitarianism*, ed. George Sher (Indianapolis: Hackett Publishing Company, 1979), p.7.
12. Ibid., p. 7.
13. Immanuel Kant, *Foundations of the Metaphysics of Morals*, ed. Lewis White Beck (Indianapolis: The Bobbs-Merrill Company, 1976), p. 9.
14. Of course, the libertarian cannot just *assert* that determinism is false. Reasons must be given both for concluding that determinism is false and for accepting the libertarian account of action. So, there are two key components to the libertarian's task.
15. The language here can be confusing. If there are causally *sufficient* conditions for action A, then action A is causally *necessitated* by those conditions. Necessary conditions may not be sufficient to necessitate the action, but sufficient conditions *do* necessitate it. If *all* of the necessary conditions are present,

then they are jointly sufficient. It may take practice to become comfortable using these terms, but the ideas they express are quite clear and are already familiar to you.

16. Maimonides, "Eight Chapters," in *Ethical Writings of Maimonides,* ed. Raymond L. Weiss (New York: Charles Butterworth, Dover Publications, 1983), p. 60.
17. Aristotle, *Nicomachean Ethics,* trans. Terence Irwin (Indianapolis: Hackett Publishing Company, 1985), p. 240.
18. Ibid., p. 239.

Chapter 4

Did I Say That?

IN THIS CHAPTER WE WILL MAKE SOME OBSERVATIONS AND suggestions about writing philosophy papers. Our aim is to bring into relief some of the distinctive aspects of writing about philosophy and to illustrate their importance.

Up to this point we have focused on the distinctive features of philosophical problems. Philosophy, though, is an activity, and reading, writing, and discussing philosophical ideas are all equally important modes of philosophical activity. You will enjoy philosophy the most when these modes are constructively intertwined. For one thing, this is a discipline in which insight and argumentation, thought in *motion,* is crucial. Saying things out loud, responding to them, revising them, and so forth is an especially effective way to learn and practice philosophy. A conversation is not just a report of what each participant thinks. It can also be part of the intellectual engine that puts and keeps thought in motion. Granted, you will do a lot of studying and wrestling with ideas on your own, yet, when you do enter into conversation about philosophical topics you will be struck by how the pace of your thinking is accelerated and by how much more relevant the ideas seem.

Discussing and reading philosophy support each other. When ideas are tested in dialogue, you can return to reading with an enlarged perspective and sharpened focus. Likewise, if you have read carefully and thoughtfully, then discussion will lead somewhere. When you read philosophy, try to keep in mind that the author is setting out to do a certain job. Philosophers are not reporting information; they are articulating their reasoning. Hence, it is a good idea to approach a reading with these questions in mind:

1. What is the central issue, or the matter in question?
2. What are the author's main claims and arguments?
3. What does the author claim to accomplish with them?
4. Does the author succeed?
5. Can I explain why this author succeeds (or fails) at the job he or she set out to do?

If you have read successfully, you will be able to some extent answer these questions.

Writing, too, is crucial in learning and doing philosophy, and it is an excellent test of whether you can answer these kinds of questions. Writing is a very effective way to show how your own thinking moves and to discover if it is keeping up with the issues you have been reading about and discussing. You want the reader of your paper to answer the questions above in certain ways rather than others. How can you make that happen? It is to be expected that you will not be quite sure about what you are supposed to do when you begin writing philosophy papers. This chapter is intended to help you.

Types of Papers

Philosophy papers are a different sort of undertaking from most kinds of writing. For example, you often do not need to do research for a philosophy paper. Sometimes instructors will insist that you *not* do research. They will want you to study your primary readings and reflect upon them and the issues they concern. Even when it is recommended that you do some research, what is crucial is to *incorporate* the arguments and insights that you find in your research into your paper. You might use it to support your own position or to criticize other authors as a way of exhibiting your skill in taking on opponents and responding to objections. What is important is that the research is used to enlarge your thinking and not just to enlarge your paper. It should become part of what you are thinking about in addressing the paper topic.

You may also occasionally do some factual research. It is always good to be factually informed when writing philosophy. If you are writing about affirmative action, you may want to get the facts about who goes to college or who enters various occupations. If you are writing about capital punishment you may want to compare statistics on serious crimes in states that have capital punishment and states that do not. The facts alone will not resolve the philosophical problems. They will, however, give you a clearer sense of what is at stake and what sorts of considerations can be effectively used in making arguments. In general, though, writing assignments in philosophy courses do not call for research. Nonetheless, a philosophy paper is generally not just a meditation about a topic. More often it is a close examination of a text or texts and the claims and arguments in them. They report the results of thought—*your thought*. That is why it is especially important to take care in writing them.

Writing is not an accessory to learning philosophy. It is a very important practice by which it is learned. In writing, you have to actually construct the sentences that articulate your thoughts and your understanding, and that is why precision, clarity, and order are of the utmost importance. Also, in writing a paper you are assuming an important kind of responsibility. When the reader reads your paper, you will not be there to say such things as, "Well, what I really meant was. . .," or "A clearer way for me to say that is. . ." Your paper may be the only record that the reader has of your thoughts.

Expository Writing

Even if the paper topic makes it quite explicit what you are to do, just the fact that it is a philosophy paper makes the project distinctive. For example, suppose you have been reading Hume's *An Enquiry Concerning Human Understanding,* and you are given a paper topic such as the following: "Write three to four pages explaining why Hume denies that the causal relation is a relation of objective necessity." There are some very famous sections of Hume's *Enquiry* on exactly this matter, so it might seem that if you have read those sections, writing the paper should not be especially challenging. This sort of paper, in which you present a philosopher's main argument, or explicate his or her main claims, is assigned quite often. This is *expository* writing. Can't you just "say what Hume said"?

The short answer is no. A summary of what an author has said is different from a philosophy paper, even if the latter is supposed to be just a reconstruction of what an author maintains. There is a discernible difference between a paper that is written with comprehension and one that consists mostly of a summary or paraphrase that reports what an author has said, but does so without philosophical understanding.

There is a very good chance that the reader of your paper already knows what the author has said. You are writing the paper in order to show that you have a grasp of the issues and the arguments that the author presents.

If you are writing about Hume's account of the idea of causal necessity, you need to state clearly what it is that he is objecting to and what his account is of the idea of necessity. You could write down a list of sentences that give an accurate summary of his main points, but that would not be a philosophy paper. Such a list could be a resource you might use as a tool to organize your thoughts. What you write should indicate that you understand the key moves the author has made and should give evidence of your philosophical engagement with the topic.

Expository writing is a test of your ability to identify a thinker's main claims and arguments in an economical manner. You may need to read a text several times and also fashion and refashion your exposition of it several times. For our sample paper topic, you want to explain that Hume maintained:

(a) that causality does not involve objective necessity
(b) that we in fact observe no more than regular patterns of temporal succession between events and
(c) that our idea of causal necessity arises from a habit of association in our minds, not from any impression of objective necessity.

These statements are accurate and could be a part of a helpful list of main points. This is not quite the same thing as a clear, economical rendering of Hume's thought on this matter. To do that, you need to explain *how* and *why* (a), (b), and (c) are among his main claims.

A helpful practice is to try to write a brief précis of a chapter or an article. It may be very brief, even just two or three sentences. Then, look it over and ask yourself if it really captures and expresses what is most important, or if it just says some stuff. Then write it again and again, if necessary. The aim of doing this is not to imprint it on your memory but to demand of yourself that you get the point and make the point as clearly and accurately as you can. This is a test of comprehension and a practice by which you gain comprehension.

Some instructors may ask that you keep a journal, something like a philosophical diary. It should be more than just a record of what you have read. Keeping such a journal is a good way to press yourself to identify and clearly state the main claim and key argument of a reading. This is also a way of monitoring how successfully you are reading.

If you walk away from a reading unable to produce that brief, to-the-point summary, you know that there is a gap that you need to fill, and you are not ready to write a paper on that material. Your writing will be made much more effective by effective reading, and vice versa. If you make it a regular practice to produce a précis of what you have read you will not only have a valuable resource, you will also get more out of your reading. You will be reading with a certain goal in mind, namely, to achieve a level of comprehension so that you can articulate what is at issue and in what way.

A philosophy paper should have a clear direction of development. It is possible to write many accurate things about a topic or an author but still fail to have written a successful paper. The work that the paragraphs do is not simply supplying content but also building a case, or tracing out a line of argument. Each of (a), (b), and (c) above merits its own paragraph, fitted into an orderly exposition. It is of the first importance that a reader come away from your paper with a clear sense of the task the paper was performing and the order in which it was performed.

A good way to imagine what counts as success is to ask yourself the following question, "Would an intelligent person, who has not just been reading the texts or studying the topics my paper covers, get a clear sense of the main issue and what I have to say about it by reading my paper *once*?" Another way to see if the right sorts of demands have been met is to read over your paper after you have finished writing it, and then see if you can outline it on the basis of reading it. Does it have a direction of development? Is the main claim or main argument clear? How coherent is the resulting outline?

Critical Writing

In addition to expository papers, you may be asked to write papers that are more critical. In these you develop objections to an argument or a theory, and you may also be expected to consider how a defender of the argument or theory might respond to your objections. This is a very instructive method of developing habits of intellectual responsibility. When you have to develop responses to your own objections, you discover very vividly how strong or weak your objections are.

Suppose your paper topic is the following: "The soft determinist view is that actions can be both causally necessitated and voluntary. Is this an incoherent view, or is there a successful defense of it? Whichever position you take, consider what would be the strongest objection to your position, and respond to that objection."

Imagine that you wish to show that soft determinism is fatally flawed. You want to argue that an action cannot be both causally necessary *and* voluntary. You hold that if an act is causally necessary then it is unavoidable, it could not be helped, and the agent could not have done otherwise. What scope is there for voluntariness? If every action is a fully determined result of a causal process over which the actor had no control, then the actor does not have control over what action to perform. It cannot be that he or she acts voluntarily.

Then you get to the part where you identify and respond to what you take to be the strongest objection to your view. Let's propose the following as the objection you discuss: "As long as we distinguish between different kinds of causes, we can see that determinism is not inconsistent with voluntary action. There is an important difference, for example, between jumping off of a diving board in order to impress someone by the side of the pool and being shoved off by surprise by someone who sneaks up behind you. In the first case, the cause of your action includes your own desires and beliefs. Given what they are, of course you jumped. You were motivated to do so. That is what makes the action voluntary and *yours*. The fact that your beliefs and desires themselves are the products of other causes makes the act no less voluntary. You jumped because you intended to. Your intentions must come from somewhere. They too are caused, yet if your actions are caused by your intentions, what more could be needed in order for them to be voluntary? So, causation, as such, does not defeat voluntariness. Only certain kinds of causes do."

Now you need to respond to this objection in a way that supports your original position. This may not be easy. The objection is a serious one, and the critique of soft determinism needs to supply an answer to it. In order for your response to be effective, you need to consider what the objector might say in response to your response. You do not need to consider every subsequent move and countermove. You do, however, want your paper to take on a worthy objector. Part of what it is to have and to defend a position is an awareness of the most important rivals to it. An important feature of learning and writing philosophy is an appreciation of the content of, and rationale for, positions other than the one you endorse. To ensure that you show that appreciation, you need to look at the topic from the objector's standpoint. That is one of the most effective ways of articulating your own view.

Sometimes when writing a paper of this sort, the paper seems to self-destruct. You present the view you wish to defend. Then you present the objection to it. You discover that it is really a quite good objection, and you wonder what to conclude. You have managed to raise serious doubts about what you wanted to show, and you are not quite sure how to get out of the difficulty. Do not feel badly about this. It is a sign that you are beginning to understand philosophical argument. It is very likely that you will feel some frustration. Try to think of it as frustration that you have *earned*. You were able to get to that point because you were able to make the moves to see that the issue is a complex and difficult one without an obvious or easy solution. Perhaps you now have reasons to change your mind about the matter and reconsider your original view. On the other hand, you might acknowledge the force of the objection to your view but still believe that the original thesis is correct, so you begin looking for other ways to answer the objection. Responding to objections allows you to progress philosophically and should be done willingly and energetically.

One avenue of response to the objection might be this: The distinction that the soft determinist makes between causation and compulsion is only superficially plausible. It leaves in place the claim that all actions are causally necessitated. If indeed they are, then it does not matter that an agent wanted to do what he did; he still could not help it. He had to do it, given the laws of nature (over which he has no control). The soft determinist's distinction does not mark the relevant sort of difference. Causation is causation, you say, and what must be, must be; so how can causally necessary actions be voluntary? If the soft determinist insists on holding on to determinism, then he will have to give up the claim that some actions are voluntary. If the soft determinist insists on holding on to voluntariness, then determinism has got to go. He cannot have it both ways.

That is not the end of the matter, of course. There are responses available to the soft determinist. Our purpose here is not to make a point about soft determinism but about writing papers. The expectation is not that you will settle the matter once and for all. Writing a critical paper of this type helps you recognize and articulate the argumentative possibilities of philosophy. At the same time, there should be a sustained focus so that the argumentative possibilities you pursue give your paper a coherent, unified direction of development and exhibit an awareness of other positions.

Argumentative Writing

There are other kinds of papers that you may be asked to write. One type of paper that is often assigned is the argumentative paper. Sometimes, even quite early in a course, you may be asked to write a paper in which you are to develop an argument in favor of or in opposition to a certain claim. When you are asked to do this early on, it can be a little intimidating; you may not feel at all confident about how to proceed. You should not let that discourage you. The point of such an assignment is not to show how deficient you are at developing arguments but to help you to find out how to do it well.

Suppose you are asked, for example, to "Develop an argument that shows that moral values are (or are not) universal and objective." What are you to do? In one respect the main elements of the task are obvious. You need to clearly identify what you wish to argue for, and you need to argue for it. When you are reading a philosophical text, you try to identify the job that the author is trying to accomplish. What is the main issue at stake? What is the author's stand on that issue? How does the author's argument make a contribution to the debate about that issue? When someone reads your paper (including you, when you are examining drafts of it or proofreading the more polished versions), it is important that the answers to those questions can be easily found. You might begin by indicating why the issue is significant and is disputed. After all, the arguments about it should *matter* in that something important is at stake. Then you should clearly assert what it is you wish to show. One reason for writing argumentative papers is to get practice at making a commitment and following through with it, in the sense of challenging yourself to figure out the best reasons for that stand on the issue rather than some other stand. Then, to the best of your ability, explain just what you mean.

Suppose you take the stand that there are objective and universal moral values. To what does that commit you? Does that mean that what is morally right and morally wrong is self-evident? Do you mean that there is innate moral knowledge? Do you mean that rational creatures can use reason to arrive at objective moral principles? Be as clear as you can about the content of your main claim, and then be as clear as you can about the reasons why someone should accept it. An argumentative paper is a little bit of an intellectual autobiography, but it is not just a report of your beliefs. Its task is to lay out the reasons for your beliefs in a manner that engages the intellectual energy of the reader and his or her own critical, reflective abilities. The reader should get a clear sense of your intentions in such a way that he or she is drawn into the debate about the issue.

Argumentative papers are also sometimes assigned later in a term (perhaps after you have done some expository and critical writing) to give you a chance to do more independent writing which is tied less to the arguments that are found in your readings. These arguments will still be important resources and will shape your thinking, but in an argumentative paper you deploy those resources in your own thinking.

Writing expository and critical papers trains you in recognizing and in making moves and in seeing where they lead, but in argumentative papers you are making your own moves.

Even when you are writing an argumentative paper, you need not feel that your discussion must lead to final closure on the topic. In general, it is important to have the right scale of ambition when setting out to write a philosophy paper. Most of the time, quite modest ambition is ambition enough. Is it at all likely that you will solve the problem of freedom of the will and determinism, the existence of God, whether there are natural kinds, or moral facts? Actually, no. That is not a criticism of your abilities. It is a fact about the difficulty and complexity of the issues. You can be very good at philosophy and at the same time be fully aware that philosophical depth can be with respect to what the problems *are*, rather than to *solving* them. As we remarked in chapter 1, there is an important difference between good reasons and bad reasons, strong arguments and weak arguments, and so forth, even if we do not achieve lasting and final resolutions of the issues we wrestle with. In an argumentative paper, you should worry less about conclusively resolving the issue, and focus your concern on the effectiveness of your argument. This is mainly a matter of clarity in what is claimed, orderliness of presentation, and awareness of what else is "out there" in the sense that you anticipate objections, attend to ambiguities, and are alert to why others see considerable merit in different positions. Very early on we noted the distinction between an opinion and a view or justified beliefs. When you write an argumentative paper, you are articulating a view, and it needs to be supportable in ways that others can recognize.

Contrastive Writing

Another type of paper you might be asked to write requires that you examine the relative merits of different philosophical positions. We shall call this a contrastive paper. For example, you might be asked to discuss and evaluate the differences between rationalism and empiricism as theories of knowledge or to critically consider Kantian and utilitarian approaches to the issue of capital punishment. To do a good job at this, try to figure out what would intellectually motivate someone to hold one or the other of these various positions.

If you are writing a paper about capital punishment, the emphasis should be on what sorts of considerations are relevant to a Kantian and to a utilitarian rather than on answering the question, "Would a Kantian (or utilitarian) be for it or against it?" They could conceivably agree that it is permissible (or not permissible), while giving very different explanations of what justifies that conclusion. The same holds for many other topics. It is the arguments that matter and the different conceptions of what is relevant evidence and how it counts towards the argument.

The contrast between philosophical positions is often a contrast between the reasons for a certain conclusion, rather than a contrast in what the conclusion is. For example, people may agree that capital punishment should be abolished, but they differ over the reasons why. One view is that capital punishment could be justified if it were shown to bring substantial benefits (in terms of deterrence, public safety, increased feelings of security, etc.), but the evidence is that it does not bring such benefits. Another view is that a civil society should not take the life of any of its members in a planned, deliberate way. To do so is to show a lack of respect for life and to raise doubts about the society's willingness to seek alternative, more constructive responses to serious crime. There are some thinkers who maintain that capital punishment is justifiable *in principle* but that it is so erratic and discriminatory in its operation that it should be abandoned. This is a problem of fairness in the conduct of the practice, rather than a doubt about the moral legitimacy of the practice in its own right. There are several others as well.

It should not be expected that different philosophical positions will always come to different conclusions. Thinkers who make different assumptions and who focus on different aspects of an issue may disagree on all of the key points, and they often do, but they do not have to. Always look to the reasoning; that's where many of the key philosophical moves are made. Recall what we said about the skeptic. The skeptic may argue that none of our beliefs are justified to the extent that they count as knowledge, yet still we carry on maintaining those beliefs, the skeptic along with the rest of us. The key points of contrast are in the *reasoning*, not just the apparent *results*.

Some of the things that are of the first importance in whatever sort of paper you are writing are:

1. Clarity about what you are setting out to accomplish and what is at stake in that topic.
2. Effective organization that leads the reader in an orderly way through the moves you make in your reasoning.
3. Awareness of objections to your view and awareness of other positions on the issues.

In the effort to achieve these goals, you will find that you may need to revise your paper more than once, paying attention to overall structure, word choice, and the formulations of your ideas.

The Importance of Multiple Drafts

It is no easier to write a philosophy paper in one draft than to master a philosophical reading in one sitting or to give an effective, well-organized philosophical presentation with no preparation. It is a very rare individual who can fully plan what to write and then just sit down and write it in a polished, finished manner. It is much more likely that you will figure out what to write *while* writing, *by* writing.

Having to write about a reading forces (or at least it should force) you to go back to it with closer attention and with a more discerning and critical eye. It is not good enough to just get an impression of a reading or an issue in the "Oh, yeah, I've heard of that" mode. If you are going to write about something, you need to really know your way around it. Likewise, it is often the case that in order to really know your way around a topic or a text in philosophy, you need to write about it. Reading and writing philosophy reinforce each other. When you are writing about a topic it may look somewhat different when you reread the texts you are writing about. This is because in writing about it, you have a definite focus of attention, and you are reading with a view to notice and examine certain things. Writing can help highlight aspects of a text that otherwise might not have stood out for you.

You may have heard people say something like "If you really want to understand something, you need to teach it." It is true that one very effective way to achieve a sound understanding of something is to explain it to others. If you have to actually formulate the sentences, say them out loud, anticipate what will be problematic or confusing, and clarify what matters about whatever it is you are explaining, you really need to know what you are talking about. Writing is much like that, and by writing, you are explaining matters to yourself as well as to the reader.

It is a good idea to read your work out loud. That way you will pay more attention to the flow of your writing and to the precision with which your ideas are expressed. Philosophy is, in large part, conversation in the sense that claims are advanced, responded to, and presented again with suitable revision, qualification, or additional justification. What you write should show that it has been thought through in that manner even if you were the sole participant in the conversation.

It is very difficult to be effective critics of our own writing. For one thing, our egos are invested in it. Also, there is generally a level of comfort with our own ways of saying things, and we do not hear them or read them in the ways that others might. Still, it is very important to try to be an honest, alert critic of your own writing. Really ask yourself if the way you have written about something would succeed in explaining it to another person. Does your writing need to be "decoded"? Are there clearer and more accurate ways of saying what you intend to say, either by exercising more care in word choice or in the organization of your paper? One of the most important things to do is to break out of the circle of your own idiom. Remind yourself that the reader may not be thinking about the subject in just the same terms that you are thinking about it. Try to use words in such a way that your meaning is as public and as accessible as you can make it. It is possible to be both sophisticated and straightforward.

You should be prepared to write multiple drafts, to discard sentences, paragraphs, and even whole pages at a time, if need be. Doing this is not a sign of failure. It is a mark of effort and ambition. Besides, before our writing becomes clear and articulate, we sometimes need to get the "gunk" out of our pipes. If you do not write rough drafts, it is likely that the gunk will still be there when you do sit down and try to write the finished version on the first attempt.

Now let's look at a brief sample passage and examine it for possible revisions. Suppose, again, that you are writing a paper on the free will and determinism issue. You are asked to briefly explain the main theses of hard determinism, libertarianism, and compatibilism and to indicate their merits and weaknesses. When you get to your explanation of compatibilism, you write, "The compatibilist position is a combination of hard determinism and libertarianism. This is because compatibilism believes that we perform free actions and that all of our actions are caused. This doesn't make any sense. Either an action is free, or it is determined. It cannot be both. The compatibilist is trying to combine things that don't go together, so the position is meaningless."

Look carefully at those six sentences. Before you go on reading here, ask yourself what revisions or corrections might be appropriate. Granted, you may not have studied these issues yet, so the topic may be somewhat unfamiliar. You can get some help by going back to the brief discussion of these positions in chapter 3 and by looking at the glossary at the end of the book. You should be able to notice some of what needs to be repaired or corrected even without specific knowledge of this topic or the literature on it.

There are several opportunities for revision in this passage. Here are some suggestions.

(1) The sentence "The compatibilist position is a combination of hard determinism and libertarianism" is false. Compatibilists maintain that determinism is compatible with free will and moral responsibility. That may sound like the original claim in the sample paper, but it is actually quite different. Remember, the hard determinist argues that determinism is inconsistent with free will and moral responsibility. According to hard determinism, *if* determinism is true, *then* there is no freedom of the will, and the hard determinist does indeed maintain that determinism is true. The libertarian argues that determinism is false and that there is freedom of will of the sort needed for moral responsibility. Hard determinism and libertarianism exclude one another. Compatibilism is a third, and different, view. It does not maintain that there is no free will, and it does not maintain that determinism is false.

(2) The phrase "Compatibilism believes . . ." is awkward. It is better to say "Compatibilists believe . . ." or "Compatibilism is the view that . . ."

(3) What about the sentence, "This doesn't make any sense."? The problem with it is that it suggests that something is wrong with the view, but it is not adequately specific. In colloquial speech we often say, "That doesn't make any sense," as a way of saying: (a) I don't believe that; (b) I don't know what you mean; (c) That doesn't fit with other things we know or believe; or (d) I cannot see the reason for that. If you intend to use the expression literally in the sample paper, then what you are saying is basically this: "Compatibilism is nonsense. The compatibilist thesis has no clear meaning." Yet, that is probably not what you intend to say. Indeed, the thesis does have a clear meaning, but you think that compatibilism is false. Its defect is not that it is meaningless or that it says nothing; what you probably mean is that its defect is that it is not true. This is an example of the importance of careful word choice. It is easy to be misinterpreted, so precision is crucial.

(4) Consider these statements, "Either an action is caused, or it is free. It cannot be both." As long as there is argumentative support for these claims, that is fine. They are not, however, *obviously* true. For one thing, another possibility is that some actions are matters of chance; they are neither causally necessitated nor exercises of libertarian freedom. It is open to the student writing the sample paper to

deny that such behavior properly counts as a human *action* at all. He does, though, need to exercise care with dilemmas of this kind. Their components may not be jointly exhaustive (covering all cases) and mutually exclusive (nothing is in both categories). Whether an action can be both free and caused is the issue on which compatibilism is a certain stand. It is unlikely that it can be demolished or dismissed so quickly. The student may be right that an action cannot be both free and determined, but that needs to be shown and not just asserted.

(5) The final sentence of the excerpt from the sample paper says that compatibilism is meaningless. To some extent, we have already been over this territory. The weakness of compatibilism in this student's view is not that the compatibilist thesis has no meaning but that it is **inconsistent**. That is expressed by, "The compatibilist is trying to combine things that don't go together . . ." If a claim is inconsistent, it contains components that cannot be true together. There may not be an obvious contradiction such as, "All actions are causally necessitated, but some have no causes." It can take some effort to discover an inconsistency. Part of the debate about human action is whether compatibilism does indeed involve an inconsistency. Being inconsistent and being meaningless are different. If compatibilism is inconsistent it is because it *is* meaningful, and its component claims cannot be true together.

The Importance of Word Choice

We have repeatedly noted the importance of precise use of language in philosophy. A great deal can hang on just how a term such as "certain," "necessary," or "good" is understood. We can illustrate the importance of precision by considering some terms that are widely used in student writing. Among them are "false," "**contradictory**," "ridiculous," "ludicrous," "**incoherent**," and "inconsistent." It is easy to fall into a habit of using one of them when another should be used because they all seem to have a similar connotation. They all indicate that something is not right, yet each has its own meaning and serves to make a distinct point.

To say that a statement or a belief is false is just to say that it is not true. Whether it is false because it is contradictory, or for some other reason, is a matter that you need to be careful about. Not every statement that is false is so because it is contradictory. "There is a group of unicorns frolicking on the moon," is false, yet not contradictory. The same goes for "The Washington Monument is taller than the Empire State Building." The statements are just factually false, unlike, "The Washington Monument is taller than anything exactly the same height as it." That is false, because it is **logically impossible** that it should be true. It is a contradictory statement.

A statement or a belief is *self*-contradictory when it both asserts and denies the same thing, and statements or beliefs contradict each other when one asserts what the other denies. Suppose, for example, someone said, "You have got to come over here and see this picture of a circle with four right angles." It cannot be the case that something is both a circle and a rectilinear figure. The notion of a rectilinear circle is a contradictory notion. Similarly, if someone says, "Napoleon was defeated at the Battle of Waterloo, which is a battle he won," that, too, would be contradictory. The assertion of one of those claims as true requires that the other is false.

That relation of truth and falsehood is also important to understanding inconsistency. What is said may not be a straightforward contradiction, but it can still involve or imply an inconsistency. For example, there are many thinkers who maintain that the following is inconsistent: "God is omnipotent, and human beings have free will." That does not look like a contradictory statement. Still, it is often argued that the claim involves or implies an inconsistency. The reason given is that *if* God is omnipotent and is the cause of everything (including all that there is, what it is like, and what it does), *then* all human action (like everything else) is caused by God's power, and there is no place for freedom of will. Or if we insist that there is freedom of the will, then there are actions that are not caused by God's power, and thus God is not omnipotent because free human actions are uncaused, even by God. It appears that the two claims asserted in the original statement are inconsistent with each other.

This is by no means the end of the issue. We should not think that we have just proved that there is an inconsistency that eliminates either free will or an omnipotent God. This question of philosophical theology cannot be dealt with conclusively in one swift paragraph. In fact, it is more like the beginning of the issue. There is work to be done in defending the view that the original claim is not inconsistent and there are replies to that defense. The point we should take note of is that a claim can involve an inconsistency or be inconsistent with other claims in ways that are not obvious and that do not involve obvious contradictions. Some careful reasoning may be needed in order to identify an inconsistency.

The issue of consistency is extremely important. Often in an argument we will be listening to what the other party to the argument is claiming, and then at some point we will say something like, "Now just a minute. Two minutes ago you said X, and now you tell me Y, but you cannot maintain *both* X and Y. They are inconsistent. So, which way do you want it?" Either the appearance of inconsistency must be explained away, or that person must revise what he or she is accepting and asserting. If a position involves inconsistency, that defeats it. The statements that are inconsistent may be far apart in the presentation of the position, but that does not diminish the inconsistency.

There are other words that you may be tempted to use which do not have narrow, technical meanings, but it is still very important to use them in precise ways. For example, what is it for a claim to be ridiculous or ludicrous? This is not a formal notion like contradiction or inconsistency. There is not a single, definite criterion for these notions, though we should exercise care in how we use them. It is not quite right to say that a statement is false because it is ridiculous. At least, you should spell out more specifically what you mean when you say that a statement is ridiculous or that it is false because it is ridiculous. Maybe it is ridiculous to believe the statement because there is no evidence for it and there is much evidence against it. That would seem to be the case with regard to the lunar unicorn statement above. Acceptance of it is ridiculous or ludicrous, and that is generally what is meant when we say that a statement is ridiculous or ludicrous; it is plain that it is false, and it is immensely improbable that it could be true. When someone tells us, "I ate fifty-eight slices of pizza in three minutes," we react by saying, "That's ridiculous," and we mean that we have excellent reasons for thinking that it is not true.

What about incoherence? This notion is used in a number of ways. Sometimes when we detect a contradiction, our assessment is, "That's incoherent." The statement is incoherent because the components do not "fit" together; they cannot be true together. Contradiction and inconsistency can make for incoherence. There are also ways of being incoherent that are not strictly matters of logical structure. Sometimes we use the notion to indicate that something is unintelligible, that it makes no sense. This second kind of incoherence is more a matter of content. When people put things into code in order to protect secrets, they want the message to be incoherent to all those who do not have knowledge of the code. If we cannot make sense of something, cannot understand what is meant despite our best efforts, it may be because it is incoherent. Consider the following: "The reason there are too many pandas in the tool chest is because no fried egg laughs in the north pressure." There is no coherent literal meaning in this sentence, though its defects are not strictly logical.

Another kind of incoherence is illustrated by the following. Suppose someone heats a quantity of fresh water (at sea level) to 150 degrees

Celsius and reports to us that it froze instead of boiled. We react by saying "That's incoherent. The change you are talking about is not permitted by the laws of nature. Either your equipment is faulty, or that is not ordinary water you are working with." Given what we know, the reported event is not (causally) possible. It does not "fit" with other claims we have overwhelming reason to accept. The statement makes literal sense and contains no formal contradiction. Still, it does not cohere with other beliefs that we have very good reasons to accept. Its lack of coherence is not internal. It is a matter of its relations with *other* claims. There is much better reason to reject this statement than to reject the others (about water, heating, boiling, and freezing) with which it does not cohere.

When you charge a philosophical claim or argument with incoherence, you are saying something quite strong about it, and you should be as specific as you can in identifying and diagnosing the incoherence. You also make a strong claim when you charge something with being ridiculous or ludicrous. Always use terms such as "incoherent" and "ridiculous" with care, and do not overcommit yourself and invite objections in this manner. Remarks such as "That's ridiculous," or "That claim is incoherent," in ordinary conversational contexts are ways of saying "I strongly disagree," or "I can prove that you are mistaken." It is very rare indeed that you will be asked to read a work of philosophy that really is incoherent in a simple way. Whatever incoherence there is will not be on the surface, and it will take some sustained philosophical investigation to find it. The overall coherence of your own claims is one of the most important aspects of writing, whatever sort of paper you are asked to write.

Some other terms that are too often used interchangeably are "true," "valid," "**sound**," "tenable," and "viable." It is incorrect to say that an argument is true (or false). "True" and "false" do not apply to arguments. They *do* apply to the premises of arguments and to their conclusions. In the argument: "All dogs are mammals, cats are dogs, therefore, cats are mammals," the first premise is true and so is the conclusion. The second premise is false. In fact, the argument is valid; its conclusion does follow from its premises as a matter of logical necessity. It is, however, an **unsound** argument. Arguments are valid or invalid (that is, in good logical form or defective logical form). They are also sound or unsound. They are sound when they are valid and they contain no false statement as either premise or conclusion. Inclusion of a false statement as premise, conclusion, or an invalid logical form is enough to render an argument unsound. It is never correct, however, to say that an argument is true or false.

Apart from the technical use of "valid" there is a nontechnical use. For example, we can correctly say that "Human beings need oxygen for respiration," is a valid statement. We can also say that something is a valid consideration as a way of saying that it is relevant and that it is appropriate to bring it up. Sometimes in the debate over capital punishment, critics claim that even if it is morally justifiable in principle, it is so erratic and discriminatory in practice that it should be ended. That might be described as a "valid" criticism. However, when said of arguments, "valid" has a very precise meaning.

A position or argument is tenable when there are grounds to support it and it stands up to objections. The word "tenable" does not have a specific technical meaning. In that respect, it differs from "valid" or "sound." An argument is untenable if it is unsound. Why it is unsound should be shown very precisely. A statement is untenable when there is clear evidence that it is false.

"Viable" is a word that is very frequently used as a general term of positive evaluation. Used in this way, it tends to lack precision. The primary meaning of "viable" is something like "capable of existing independently or on its own." For example, a newborn who does not need any life-support equipment is viable. Or, we might say, "The settlement was located in a wilderness area, but it produced enough food to be viable." Try not to use "viable" as a catchall term, doing the various jobs of "valid," "sound," "tenable," or various other terms. Use the term that means just what you mean, and say what you mean as clearly as you can.

Hey, There Aren't Any Pictures

One of the most effective ways to show that you understand the concepts and issues you are writing about is to develop detailed illustrations. Illustrations are a way to show how and why philosophical claims are of real importance. An example can often clarify a point or drive it home so that the response of the reader is, "Oh, *now* I see what you mean." Good illustrations are not mere accessories. They are important to the effective development and presentation of philosophical ideas. It takes skill to construct really effective illustrations, and it takes imagination and practice to acquire the skill.

If you take more courses in philosophy, you will find that there are some illustrations that have become landmarks, marking key issues or purported solutions to them. A really good illustration can become a focus of argumentative attention, and reference to it can be used as a signal of your position. These may not mean much to you now, but if you go on in philosophy, it is quite likely that you will meet with **Hilary Putnam's** (1926–) "twin earth"[1] example, **Bernard Williams'** (1929–) "Jim and the Indians"[2] example, and **Saul Kripke's** (1940–) "meter stick"[3] example. These are all examples from quite recent philosophy. Other examples, ones that have been enduring, some for over twenty centuries, are Plato's Euthyphro[4] example, Aristotle's "throwing cargo overboard in a storm"[5] example, and Descartes' "evil demon"[6] example. They are emblematic of certain philosophical issues and are referred to again and again in philosophical literature.

An illustration should be genuinely illuminating and part of the development of your view. Trying to construct an illustration is a way of finding out if you really do grasp what you are writing about and if you really are succeeding in articulating your view.

For example, suppose you are writing a paper about the justification of punishment. This is a topic about which people often have quite strong views. Many people believe that the reason to punish wrongdoers is that they *deserve* to be punished. Justice, it is often held, requires that if someone is guilty of wrongdoing, then punishment is deserved. This view is **retributivism**. This position maintains that guilt (not the feeling, but the fact of being guilty) is both necessary and sufficient for justifying punishment of a criminal offense whether or not there is any benefit to society or to the person punished. In your paper you want to show the weakness of the case for pure retributivism and that retributivism on its own is not an adequate justification for punishment.

How might you illustrate this? One possibility is the following. You could say, "Imagine that a thoroughly bad man has committed a very serious crime, the murder of an entire family, in the course of robbing them. This man is unrepentant and feels no remorse. He scoffs at the laws and at the court by which he has been convicted, and while he regrets having been caught, his conscience does not bother him. He knows that he broke the law, and his murderous act was voluntary and carried out knowingly. He was neither insane nor subject to any sort of coercion. He knows that he will be punished, but his character will not be affected by punishment. It cannot be expected to improve him."

You might then argue, "What good would it do to punish him just because he is guilty and deserves to be punished? We have supposed that punishment will not change him for the better. If we say that at least society is protected if he is imprisoned, that is not a retributivist consideration. That is a consideration about social benefit. If we say that at least the relatives and friends of the victims will feel better knowing that the murderer is being punished, that, too, is not a retributivist consideration. The same holds with regard to the notion that society cannot let criminals escape punishment for their wrongs. If the reason for this is that the fabric of society would deteriorate and that confidence in the law and the courts would be eroded, that is a reason based upon the consequences of punishment. So, on pure retributivist grounds, it seems that punishing this man would just be pointlessly harming him. It would be returning evil for evil, period. What good is that? There are reasons to punish him (such as some or all of the ones we have mentioned, and possibly others), but they are not pure retributivist reasons. The fact that he is a menace or that society needs an orderly manner in which to express its outrage are important facts that can support punishment. There is no place for pure retributivism. If we alter the facts of the case and allow that punishment might improve him, that is still a nonretributivist rationale. It should be clear that a justification for punishment cannot be given on pure retributivist grounds."

There is "your" illustration. Look it over carefully and see what you think. By describing a situation in some detail, you can make your argumentative moves clearer and show the ways in which they apply to the matter at issue. Descartes opened the *Meditations* with what are now famous thought experiments. These, too, were illustrations by which he made crucial philosophical moves. They were not merely ornamental.

A good illustration can sometimes illuminate several points at once and indicate the relations between a number of concepts. For example, the illustration in our discussion of retributivism included many of the concepts and issues involved in the debate about punishment. In the process of developing skill at constructing illustrations, it is likely that you will produce a few clunkers. One way in which illustrations often fail is that they are not developed in adequate detail. Then there is the risk that the illustration can be used for purposes other than those you designed it to serve. It could be turned against you. You want your illustration to work for you in a specific way and not to be turned into a counterexample to your view. This does not mean that you should "stack the deck"; your illustrations should be plausible, and their appeal should not be designed solely for the reader who already agrees with you.

For example, suppose you make the claim that capital punishment is wrong, and one reason for thinking that it is wrong is that mistaken executions cannot be rectified. To illustrate this, you tell the story of an actual case of mistaken conviction and execution, or you give a plausible description of one that you create yourself. The reader or objector might respond that if your worry is really about *mistakes,* then it is not really a worry about the wrongness of capital punishment but about wrong convictions. Everyone shares (or should share) concern about mistaken convictions; that is not unique to opponents of capital punishment. You might seem to be suggesting that there is nothing problematic about executing guilty people. Though that is not your view, the way you have illustrated your view leaves it open to problematic interpretation. The illustration you have given has been turned back on you in a way that weakens your argument.

A similar weakness in a paper is the use of a passage from an author to make or reinforce a point, when the quoted passage actually makes a different (possibly contrary) point. That is a sign that the person who wrote the paper was reaching and was not really in command of his or her own discussion. Suppose you are reading an article by an author who is defending libertarianism. In the course of the article, the author considers some of the determinist's objections to libertarianism. The author wants to bring these out clearly in order to try to challenge them and to show that, indeed, libertarianism can be successfully defended. At one point in the article the author writes: "The libertarian view is that free actions are not sufficiently caused by anything, not even the agent's character and the circumstances of action. This means that a free action is just a bolt out of the blue and no different from random or capricious action. An action of this kind is no different from the agent just finding himself moving this way or that way, without being guided by intention or purpose. If, to the libertarian, determinism seems to render us puppets or automata, libertarianism renders our actions mere spontaneous motions, unconnected to character or deliberation."

That sentence does not express the view of its author. It is part of the (determinist) view the author is rejecting. It is something the author says, but it is not something the author *affirms*. By misusing it to support the libertarian position, you have weakened the position you wish to defend. It is easier than you might suspect to make this sort of error of misplaced attribution. This is because authors will often present views opposed to their own with energy and care as a way of showing what belongs to the opposing position. Be cautious about just who is doing the talking when an author proceeds in this manner.

Do You Want My Opinion?

This question may be at the forefront of your mind when writing a philosophy paper. The answer is almost always "yes" in one sense and also "no" in another sense. It is "yes" in the sense that the instructor wants your paper to be a presentation of your own thought. Even if it is a paper in which you have been asked to summarize a philosopher's position or argument, you need to do your own thinking in order to succeed. A summary is not just a matter of leaving out some things, and it can be difficult to produce a good summary. At the same time, when you are writing a philosophy paper you are not just presenting your opinion. In chapter 1, we remarked on the difference between an opinion and a view. We said that a view is a reasoned position, unlike an opinion, which may be thoughtless or spontaneous. It may turn out that upon reflection, your considered view and your original opinion coincide. The difference is that when your opinion is worked into a view, you have grounds for it, and you have given some thought to its implications and presuppositions.

Expressions such as "My view is that. . . ," "To my mind. . . ," or "I think that. . . ," are sometimes appropriate. (Some instructors, however, may encourage you to *never* use them.) Use of the first person can occasionally be fine, as long as the first person has something interesting and important to say. What matters most is that the way in which you articulate your thinking is accessible to the reader. Always try to write as clearly, economically, and in as well-organized a manner as you can. Instead of writing something such as "It seems to me that Descartes' argument in the third meditation for the existence of God fails, and here is why I think so," you might write, "Descartes' argument for the existence of God in the third meditation fails for the following reasons." Then just go on and spell out the reasons. In writing philosophy papers, it is your thoughts that count, but what makes them good ones are the reasons for them.

Paper assignments that ask you to evaluate or assess a reading or an argument sound like invitations to present your own view. Indeed, they are. For example, suppose you are asked to evaluate an article on the topic of abortion, and the author of the article makes a case for wide permissibility of abortion. She maintains (for reasons that are supplied in the article) that most abortions during the first trimester of pregnancy are morally permissible. We will not, right here, try to recreate this author's reasons. Let's imagine that you do not share the author's view, and you are not convinced by the author's argument. If you are just asked to indicate your own opinion, that is one thing, but in a philosophy paper it would not be appropriate to say things such as, "This author is completely wrong because it is obvious that a human fetus is a person, and it is wrong to kill people." Why would this be inappropriate?

For a start, consider the claim, "It is wrong to kill people." If that is true, it is an appropriately defended or qualified version of it is which is true. After all, there do seem to be permissible cases of killing people. Perhaps self-defense permits it, or war, if it is killing unjust aggressors and it is in defense of a just cause. Maybe there are other reasons that permit killing human beings. What you probably mean in saying, "It is wrong to kill people," is something like, "It is wrong to kill innocent people," "It is wrong to kill a person just to enable oneself to more effectively pursue one's own aims and interests," or perhaps "A person has a right to life that is violated by abortion." This last candidate raises complex and difficult issues about the grounds and content of rights and also about who possesses them. You need to say a good deal more in order for this claim to enter into the dispute in a genuine and constructive way. Even if you believe that there are excellent reasons for why it is wrong to kill a person, ever, even in war or in self-defense, you owe it to the reader to give those reasons.

Also, the issue of whether a human fetus is a person, and just what that entails, is one of the most controversial aspects of the abortion issue. There is sharp disagreement over this, and it just is not obvious that a fetus is (or is not) a person. One view holds that a fetus is a human organism but not yet a person with interests and rights. Another regards a fetus as a *potential* person and, as such, it merits certain kinds of protection. In yet another view a fetus is *merely* a potential person, so it does not (at least at certain points of fetal life) merit the protections accorded to persons. There are still other views, each with its own plausible supporting considerations.

Moreover, it is not obvious what the answer to the question of fetal personhood should count for. This is because even if a human fetus is a person, there is still scope for argument about the permissibility of abortion. Maybe you *are* right. Perhaps on the best account that can be given, a human fetus is indeed a person, and there are sufficiently strong reasons to conclude that abortion should not (or in most types of cases, should not) be permitted. Still, even if that is the most morally sound and best justified view, what makes it so needs to be articulated. In writing, we need to remind ourselves that we cannot always expect others to assign the same weight to considerations that we do and that others may not even take the same things to be relevant considerations. When there is that sort of gap between participants in a discussion, or between author and reader, there is a great deal of room for misunderstanding. It is better to present compelling reasons for a claim than just to assert that the claim is obviously true.

Beginnings and Endings

There is nothing wrong with coming right out and saying what your main claim is and doing so near the beginning of the paper. You may be reluctant to do this, fearing that in the introductory paragraph you will have said all you have to say. To keep that from happening, maybe you write a few paragraphs before the main thesis of the paper emerges. This is generally not a good strategy. You can identify your main thesis or focus very early on and still have plenty to say. Remember, the reader is seeing this paper for the first time, and, unlike you, the reader does not know what is coming, so an opening that clearly points the way is welcome.

Give the reader a sense of what he or she is getting into and a sense of what to look for. If, near the beginning of your paper, you write something such as, "The main claim I wish to defend is. . ." you have not spoiled the drama of your paper. Plenty lies ahead for the reader, including the presentation of the reasons in support of that claim, the consideration of objections to it, and responses to those objections. Identify a focus or a main theme that retains its status throughout the paper. When you are proofreading your work make sure that each paragraph makes a contribution to the paper's thesis. Try not to give the reader the opportunity to write "start here" three paragraphs into the paper. We often have to write for a while in order to find out just what it is we are trying to say, but that material belongs in drafts and not in the opening paragraphs of the finished paper.

There are also certain things to keep in mind about writing conclusions. Recall that we looked at why it is a mistake to describe compatibilism as a combination of determinism and libertarianism (or, worse yet, a combination of hard determinism and libertarianism). That is one kind of compromise that should be guarded against. In papers on ethical theory, for example, you might wish to argue that there are flaws in Mill's utilitarian theory and there are flaws in Kant's deontological theory, so maybe the thing to do is to combine the best elements of both. That will not work. If you understand what makes Mill's theory a utilitarian theory and what makes Kant's theory a deontological theory, then you understand that at the most fundamental level there are some differences that cannot be reconciled by consensus or compromise. Their conceptions of the very phenomena addressed by moral theorizing are different in crucial ways.

This is not to say that it is impossible to formulate a plausible moral theory that in certain respects involves deontological considerations and that in certain respects involves considerations of utility. That, however, is a task of theory-construction that needs to be carried out; we cannot just "announce" that the solution to the problems of moral theory is to combine what seems best in each of a number of different theories. For instance, just as compatibilism is not a combination of determinism and libertarianism, neither is a virtue-centered approach to ethics a combination of deontology and utilitarianism.

Another common pitfall of writing is to be off-hand or too casual in the conclusions to your papers. Too often, a paper is concluded in something like the following manner: "Thus, we can see that the problem of ______ has been debated for centuries, and it probably always will be." The last sentence or paragraph of a paper is just as fully a part of the paper as any other sentence or paragraph, and like the others, it should do some work. The sentence above does not do any work. It might be the sentence with which the paper ends, but it is not really a conclusion. Following it with: "The disagreement cannot be resolved, and anyway, who is to say?" would make the situation worse, not better. When you say something such as, "The disagreement cannot be resolved," that is not just a "by the way" remark. It is a strong, substantive claim, and it needs to be supported. By all means include it, if you believe you have good reasons to support it. Otherwise, it has no place in the paper.

The very last clause, the "Who is to say?" clause, is equally unhelpful. There is, to be sure, a sense in which it might be true; after all, there are questions that may never be answered in a conclusive way. However, "Who is to say?" sounds like an abandonment of ambition and effort. It can also have the connotation that any position on the matter is just as good as any other. That is immensely implausible and to conclude your discussion in this way makes it sound as though you are dismissing the seriousness or difficulty of the issue rather than grappling with it. One answer to the question, "Who is to say?" is, "We are; the ones who engage in rigorous, critical thought." (That includes you.) You do not want your conclusion to diminish the significance of your own efforts.

For many papers there is nothing wrong with a conclusion that does not claim to solve the problem or to reconcile the opponents in the controversy. Your paper may be very successful in the respect that it shows a good understanding of the issues and the positions and a thoughtful and careful grasp of the argumentative moves. Even when you are asked to indicate a commitment to one position on an issue, you are being asked to indicate what position you believe is the best supported and most plausible, and this is not the same as being asked to solve the problem once and for all. We are often tempted to go in for the sorts of conclusions that we have just been criticizing. It is best to resist that temptation. It is always better to write an honest conclusion than to contrive a happy ending.

But It Was in My Notes

There is one sort of paper that an instructor will recognize almost immediately. This is the paper that is really not much more than a compilation of class notes. It is one of the least flattering types of papers to read. Many students rely very heavily on note-taking as a strategy of learning. For some, this works very well; good class notes can be a very valuable resource, but they are a resource only. You must make something of them by doing fresh thinking and by articulating ideas and formulating arguments in your own terms. Of course, there may be certain definitions or phrases that your instructor wishes you to use in quite specific ways. Still, those preferred formulations are to be fitted into a paper that is a record of your own thought. When you rely too heavily on class notes it is unclear to the instructor whether you really have a sound grasp of what you are writing about. It might be seen as evidence of the fact that you are very skilled at working in a stenographic mode when what the instructor is looking for is evidence of something quite different. Have *you* started to work with the ideas and the issues in a way that is original, even though you are studying the thinking of others? We sometimes have the worry, "What could I possibly add to this discussion that has not already been said?" Humility is in order, given the difficulty of the issues and the depth of the authors. Still, that should not prevent you from tackling the issues and the texts so that you develop and present your own understanding.

Paying too much attention to taking notes can sometimes have an effect opposite of what you intend. When you look over your notes you may find that you have written down a great deal, but you do not really understand it much better than if you had not written it down. Sometimes in class, I will ask students *not* to write something down if I think it is especially important. Everyone can then devote complete attention to listening, thinking about it, and reacting to it. It is harder to think of questions about what you are hearing if you are preoccupied with writing it down. Notes are not "prefabricated thoughts." They indicate matters to focus on, supply a record of what you need to examine further, help you in the use of key terms, and so forth. They need to be worked into a more finished product by your own thinking and your own efforts at articulation and argumentation.

While notes can be helpful, the process of actually writing your paper requires you to go well beyond what you may have written down in class. This is not a matter of doing research but of pursuing avenues of thought. You might feel that at least if you went and looked at some books on the relevant philosophers and topics, you would feel you had your feet planted a bit more firmly on the ground. There is, though, a good reason why you are often not expected to do research. The aim of most philosophy paper assignments is to increase your understanding of what the issues are, rather than to explore and evaluate the wider literature on them. If you rely on secondary sources, you run the risk of not really writing a philosophy paper but, instead, writing a paper that reports what some philosophers think. Worry less about what sort of information you can gather, and concentrate on developing your own thinking.

Later on, if you pursue the study of this discipline at a higher level, you will find a great deal of value in reading widely in the secondary literature, and note-taking on secondary readings may become more important. You will be able to read them critically, and make better judgments about what sorts of notes to take, because you will already have your own grasp of the issues and familiarity with some of the most important moves and positions. It is best, though, to learn them for yourself by grappling with your assigned texts and not relying on secondary sources. Otherwise, the use of secondary sources runs the risk of being too much like writing your paper on the basis of someone else's notes. You will lack fluency with them and perhaps lack the kind of control over ideas that is essential to a good paper. If you are not able to explain in your own words something that you have written, particularly if it is borrowed from another author, it does not belong in your paper. Also, when you borrow from or paraphrase sources you have consulted, you must acknowledge them in the appropriate way.

Even if your course is an introductory level course, your paper can be an excellent paper—if it is clear, orderly, and intellectually ambitious. Mistakes are welcome, if they are the result of energy rather than the lack of it. A paper need not be perfect or error-free; it needs to be a serious attempt at your own thinking.

In My Other Course We Learned . . .

Earlier, we noted that philosophy is always philosophy of something. We observed that you can no more just do philosophy without a subject matter, than you can just try, without trying to do some specific thing. While philosophy has its own distinctive way of formulating and addressing issues, it has crucial points of contact with many different disciplines and kinds of experience. You may, for example, find connections between what you study in philosophy and what you study in psychology, where you might encounter theories of motivation, personality, and moral development. Also, themes such as the nature of the self, human freedom, and morality are common to philosophy as well as to sociology, religion, and literature.

You will almost certainly find that some of the same issues are studied, though in different ways, in your philosophy courses and your other courses. Many of the issues in philosophy of mind are being addressed in neuroscience and in work on artificial intelligence. Debate about whether the human social world is properly studied by the same methods and explanatory strategies used to study the natural world is a key issue in social sciences such as sociology. In philosophy you might discuss arguments for the existence of God, while in your sociology class, you study theories of the social function of religion and the origin of religious belief.

It can be gratifying and encouraging to find these commonalities. Philosophy will seem less "cut off" and more relevant, and you will begin to appreciate the value of relating your different studies and seeing how they are attempts, in different ways, to understand many of the same things. At the same time, you might feel certain kinds of dilemmas about what to say in your philosophy papers.

This happens when an issue that is regarded by philosophers as open, contested, and still in need of analysis is addressed in one of your other courses in what seems to be a conclusive way. For example, in sociology you may encounter the view that religious belief arose from a prescientific attempt to make sense of the world and that the idea of an almighty God was a way for a people to feel that their cultural norms had objective authority. These are accounts of religious beliefs in terms of the needs felt by the human psyche, the function of shared moral norms in maintaining social cohesion, and the like. When you are asked to write a philosophy paper about arguments for the existence of God, you may feel torn about how to go about it. You are being asked to examine arguments concerning the existence of God as though the matter is not yet settled, while in your sociology course, it seems that the matter has been resolved.

What should you do? One option is to try to write the sort of paper that you think your instructor "wants" you to write, but that is not a good option. You should expect your instructor to evaluate your paper on the basis of its merits as a philosophy paper and not as a reflection of the instructor's own views of specific topics.

Another, and preferred, way to handle the dilemma is philosophically. Consider the explanations and theories that you are studying in your other subjects with some critical attention. Can you see ways in which they really *do* seem to be relevant to the philosophical issues and vice versa? Can you see ways in which they claim more than they actually deliver? Maybe there is some important distinction, or some important assumption, which has been left unexamined. Recall what we were saying back in chapter 1 about how there are always philosophical dimensions to issues, even if the relevant sciences have reached a high level of maturity and achievement.

Maybe you are reading Freud on religion, Skinner on human behavior, or E. O. Wilson on morality. Each of these, just to cite three familiar examples, is a tremendously influential thinker who has made claims about exactly the sorts of issues that philosophers work on. Each has argued that the results of scientific inquiry "solve" some fundamental, long-standing philosophical problem. It is best to take their claims very seriously and examine them with respect but also with unafraid critical rigor. Perhaps you feel that you are not in a position to do that. *They* are the authorities. They are indeed authorities, but they are not above or beyond question. In fact, trying to clarify why a theory really does seem to you to solve a philosophical problem, or why you feel that a theory must be false, can be a very effective way of finding and articulating your own philosophical position. Real explanations offered by real people are grist to the mill of philosophy. They are philosophy's crucial links to experience and to scientific inquiry and are crucial materials for philosophical thinking to work with and to work on.

The more you know about what is going on in the sciences, the arts, and the world generally, the more you will be alive to the reality of philosophical issues. You should not feel that because a theory is from a discipline other than philosophy it should not be discussed or referred to in a philosophy paper. At the same time, you should not feel that philosophical thinking is just a kind of play-acting or an intellectual indulgence that people would give up if they just paid more attention to common sense and to the sciences, where the "real" work gets done. There are different kinds of real work, and philosophy is one of them. We should neither be dismissive of what is "merely" empirical, nor should we be intimidated by the sciences. The "we" is not just "we philosophers," it is anyone who takes seriously intellectual responsibility.

Where We Are Now

There is probably no better practice than writing by which to develop habits of intellectual responsibility. In philosophical writing, clarity of expression and coherence of presentation count especially heavily. The very nature of the discipline is such that rigorous articulation can make all of the difference between understanding and success on the one hand, and confusion and frustration on the other. As we observed, it is often by writing that we work out our thinking.

Writing is also an excellent way to discover how effectively you have been reading, and writing can help you become a better reader of philosophy. When you are reading, think about what you are reading in terms of how you would write a very brief synopsis of it. If you read with the intention of doing that, you will be reading in a more directed, focused way. If you cannot write the synopsis, you need to go back to the reading. Similarly, you should strive to write in such a way that a reader of your work could briefly, clearly state "what happened" in your paper. What should happen in your paper is that an orderly development of reasoning on a definite issue is presented.

Philosophical thought is a way of achieving abstract perspective on fundamentals while at the same time attending to detail. You should see writing as part of the project of learning to think philosophically and as a crucial test of your grasp of the language and argumentative moves of philosophy. Writing philosophy papers and keeping your own journal of philosophical thoughts and summaries of readings is a way to get "inside" philosophy and to begin *doing* it rather than just reading or talking about it. As you become more comfortable and more skilled, you will find that in writing philosophy you compose your own map of the terrain, bringing certain things into relief, following certain routes, and connecting different places by your own explorations.

You may recall that in chapter 1 we discussed the question, "What good is philosophy?" This is almost like asking, "What good is disciplined thinking?" Even if you are not especially moved by the grand, enduring philosophical issues, the skills that you develop in studying philosophy will make you a more effective reader, a more effective writer, and a clearer, sharper thinker overall. Philosophical issues will better enable you to come to grips with whatever it is that interests you and whatever you undertake in life.

The Last Word

We have discussed the ways in which philosophical thought is often motivated by familiar, concrete concerns, and we have surveyed key features of some fundamental philosophical issues, ways in which they are connected, and strategies for engaging them. Philosophical thought is not a substitute for the empirical sciences, but neither are its questions answered by them. Philosophical methods are needed to address philosophical questions. Perhaps our experiences and our modes of inquiry are not directly changed by philosophy, but we are. When we study philosophy, we are doing much more than enlarging our stock of beliefs by learning new information about a subject. We are also exploring dimensions of the intellectual landscape that before we did not even notice. The demands of philosophical thought enlarge our self-knowledge by relentlessly challenging us to answer the most basic questions about reality, thought, language, and their relations. We find out where we stand and if that is a place that will support us. The problems of philosophy will outlast us and our attempts to solve them, but it is a marvelous thing to participate in something so enduring. It is both humbling and elevating in a manner all its own.

Some Things to Think About and Discuss

1. Take a look at the editorial page of a newspaper or a major news magazine and select a piece that is plainly arguing for a certain position on an issue. Examine the piece carefully. Look for unclear or misleading use of language and for errors in reasoning. Can you think of ways to reinforce the author's argument? Can you think of decisive objections to it? How might the author respond to your objection? How would you present your own position on the issue?
2. Write a brief argument defending the position that each person should be guaranteed a certain minimum level of health care at public expense. Your argument should be no more than a page in length. Compare your reasoning to the reasoning offered by others in the class. How well do the different considerations fit together into one coherent overall view? How compelling is the reasoning? After all, even the strongest case might be vulnerable to damaging objections. What are the most important objections to the argument?

3. Look carefully at the following paragraph:

For centuries people with no faith in God have made arguments that God does not exist. These arguments don't work. For one thing, God is infinite and beyond nature and human comprehension. The fact that some people do not believe that God exists is just more evidence of the weakness of the human mind and our susceptibility to error. It is often claimed that the existence of evil and suffering is proof that God does not exist. The idea is, why would God allow all of this suffering if He is perfect and omnipotent? That objection is easy to answer. The existence of evil is a test of faith and part of God's providential plan for the world. Maybe we can't understand God's reasons for allowing suffering and evil, but we shouldn't expect to understand them. It does not mean that He does not have good reasons. Also, it is just wrong to think that there is a scientific explanation for everything and that science has all the answers. Science can't explain why there is something rather than nothing. Only religion can answer that question, so that is a reason to believe in God.

How effective is this paragraph at defending the claim that God exists? Are the inferences (the steps in reasoning) clear and free of fallacies? Are the responses to objections effective? Are there ways in which word choice could be improved or in which the use of certain terms could be clarified? What assumptions are made by the author of the argument? Can you think of ways to strengthen the argument?

Key Philosophers and Texts

Aristotle (384–322 B.C.) *Nicomachean Ethics*: Aristotle's account of voluntary action and responsibility remains important to the current debate.

René Descartes (1596–1650) *Meditations on First Philosophy*: The three-stage "method of doubt" in the first meditation set the stage for a great deal of subsequent epistemological argument and theorizing.

Saul Kripke (1940–) *Naming and Necessity*: Kripke's work in logic and metaphysics is among the most influential in contemporary philosophy. He defends a version of essentialism.

Plato (429–347 B.C.) *Euthyphro*: This dialogue is a key work in the history of theorizing about the nature of ethical value, and the "Euthyphro problem" remains a central issue.

Hilary Putnam (1926–) *Reason, Truth and History*: Putnam's critique of realism has been at the center of recent debates in metaphysics, epistemology, and philosophy of language.

Bernard Williams (1929–) *Utilitarianism: For and Against*: Williams has been a forceful critic of both Utilitarianism and Kantian moral theory. He has done important work on the nature of moral objectivity and the role of character in ethical reasoning.

Endnotes

1. Hilary Putnam, *Reason, Truth and History* (New York: Cambridge University Press, 1981), see chapter 1.
2. Bernard Williams, "A Critique of Utilitarianism" in J. J. C. Smart and Bernard Williams, *Utilitarianism For and Against* (New York: Cambridge University Press, 1973), pp. 98–99.
3. Saul Kripke, *Naming and Necessity* (Cambridge: Harvard University Press, 1972), see especially pp. 22–70.
4. Plato, *Euthyphro* in *Five Dialogues*, trans. G. M. A. Grube (Indianapolis: Hackett Publishing Company, 1981), pp. 5–22.
5. Aristotle, *Nicomachean Ethics*, trans. Terence Irwin (Indianapolis: Hackett Publishing Company, 1985), Bk. III, chap. 1.
6. René Descartes, *Meditations on First Philosophy*, 3rd ed., trans. Donald A. Cress, (Indianapolis: Hackett Publishing Company, 1993), See especially Meditation One, (pp. 13–17)

Glossary

This glossary includes key terms that are used in this text. It is not intended to be a complete philosophical glossary. Also, while I have tried to make each entry accurate and clear, remember that many of these terms refer to issues that are themselves disputed, and the correct interpretation of many of these terms is itself a philosophical matter.

agent-causality: The view that agents (such as human beings) have the power to undertake action without being caused to do so. If there is agent-causality, then an agent can be the cause of its own action.

analytic philosophy: A method (and a tradition) of philosophy in which rigorous analysis of the logical structure of claims and arguments is central. Analytic philosophers often focus on very close examination of language and the way in which logical structure may be disguised by language.

antirealism: A collection of views about the relation between mind, language, and world. If one is an antirealist about some matter (for example, moral value, or causality) then one holds that what is referred to does not exist independently of how it is conceptualized or described.

compatibilism: The view that causal determinism is compatible with free will and moral responsibility. Some compatibilists hold that determinism *is* true; others hold that *even if* it is true, it is compatible with free will and moral responsibility.

consequentialism: A position in moral theorizing. The consequentialist holds that value is found in states of affairs, the outcomes or consequences of actions.

contradiction: A contradiction both asserts and denies the same thing and therefore cannot possibly be true.

deontology: A position in moral theorizing. The deontologist maintains that the central notion of morality is the notion of duty and interprets moral requirements in terms of duties and correlative rights.

determinism: The claim that all events are fully and uniquely determined such that whatever happens could not be otherwise, given what occurred prior to it.

egoism: Psychological egoism is the view that people *in fact* act only and always on the basis of what they take to be their self-interest. Ethical egoism is the view that people *should* act only and always on the basis of what they perceive to be their self-interest. Psychological egoism is an empirical hypothesis, while ethical egoism is a normative position.

epistemology: The branch of philosophy that examines the possibility, nature, and scope of knowledge.

essentialism: The view that there are certain properties that are essential to objects (or to kinds of objects) such that the objects (or kinds) could not exist without those properties. Essentialists argue that what is essential to an object (or kind) is independent of how we classify and describe things.

event-causality: The view that causality is always a relation between events and that there are no agents which exercise agent-causality.

existentialism: A number of philosophical theses and methods that focus on the nature of human existence and the way in which questions of value, the meaning of life, and human activity depend ultimately upon free human choices and commitments.

fallacy: A fallacy is an error in reasoning or an argument which commits an error in reasoning. There are formal fallacies that are matters of defective logical form, and there are informal fallacies of many kinds. Many of them concern ambiguity in the use of terms and questions of the relevance of the premises to the conclusion.

hard determinism: The view that determinism is true and that, because it is true, there is no free will.

hedonism: A theory of value that maintains that pleasure is what has intrinsic value.

incoherent: A statement or a collection of statements is incoherent when it makes no literal sense or lacks intelligible structure or relations.

inconsistent: Statements are inconsistent with each other when they cannot be true together.

induction: Reasoning in which the conclusion is supported by the premises but not logically necessitated by them.

innate: Some philosophers have held that there is innate knowledge in the sense that certain ideas or principles are part of the very constitution of the mind, so there is knowledge which is not acquired in experience.

invalid: An argument is invalid when it includes a defect in logical form so that the conclusion does not follow from the premises.

libertarianism: The view that determinism is false, that compatibilism is false, and that human beings have free will because they are agents.

logical form: The logical form of an argument or statement is its structure. Logical form can be identified and evaluated independent of the subject matter of the argument or statement.

logically impossible: A state of affairs is logically impossible when there are no conditions (actual or possible, here, there, or anywhere) in which it could be the case.

metaethics: A branch of philosophy that examines the language and concepts of morality and the methods of moral theorizing. It is not concerned directly with moral questions but with the concepts and theories that address them.

moral cognitivism: The view that moral claims are cognitive claims. There are objective moral considerations that make moral claims true or make them false.

natural kinds: If you maintain that there are natural kinds, you hold that there are real distinctions between kinds in nature and that our classifications can be guided by those real distinctions.

naturalism: The view that philosophical issues can be successfully addressed by the methods of the sciences.

necessary condition: If X is a necessary condition of Y, then Y cannot be true (or occur) unless X is true (or occurs).

necessity (causal, logical, metaphysical): If something is necessary then it must be so. If it is causally necessary then it must happen, given the laws of nature. If it is logically necessary then it is impossible that it not be the case, or it is the case no matter what else is the case. If something is metaphysically necessary it must be the case, given the natures of things, but it may not be provable as necessary on exclusively formal, logical grounds.

normative: Normative matters are matters that concern value.

primary quality: A primary quality is a property of an object that it has in its own right, independently of how we perceive it or think about it.

realism: A realist maintains that the matter at issue (for example, the existence of moral values or causality) is independent of how we conceptualize and describe it.

retributivism: The basic idea of retributivism is that guilt (wrongdoing, not the feeling of guilt) is a necessary and a sufficient condition for punishment. The retributivist claims that punishment is justified by being deserved, rather than on the basis of what benefits it might bring about.

secondary quality: A secondary quality is a property of an object (such as color or taste) that is perceived by one or another sense faculty, and the way in which it is perceived (say, as red or as bitter) does not resemble the way in which it is present in the object.

skepticism: The basic, common theme of skeptical positions is that there are grounds for doubting knowledge claims. (One may be a skeptic about all knowledge claims, or a skeptic only about knowledge claims in a certain area, for example, morality.)

soft determinism: The view that determinism is true and that it is compatible with free will and moral responsibility.

sound: An argument is sound when it is valid and its premises are true. We are then assured that the argument's conclusion is true.

sufficient condition: If X is a sufficient condition for Y, then Y is true (or occurs) if X is true (or occurs).

utilitarianism: A type of consequentialist moral theory according to which an action is right if it maximizes utility or happiness.

valid: An argument is valid when its conclusion follows necessarily from its premises.

virtue: In moral theorizing, a virtue is a characteristic of an agent that is needed in order to act well and to lead an excellent life. There are moral theorists who interpret moral issues in terms of the virtues required to have correct ethical judgment, rather than interpreting them in deontological or consequentialist terms.

Index

A

B

C

EN = Endnote